EDUCATING ENGLISH LEARNERS
FOR A
TRANSFORMED WORLD

Virginia P. Collier and Wayne P. Thomas

DUAL LANGUAGE EDUCATION OF NEW MEXICO

ALBUQUERQUE, NM   FUENTE PRESS   **FUENTE PRESS**

DUAL LANGUAGE EDUCATION OF NEW MEXICO
FUENTE PRESS

1309 Fourth St. SW, Suite E
Albuquerque, NM 87102
www.dlenm.org

©2009 by Virginia P. Collier and Wayne P. Thomas
Second printing: 2014

Library of Congress Control Number: 2009939808

ISBN 978-0-9843169-0-8

10 9 8 7 6 5 4 3 2

DEDICATION

To Cathy, Karyn, Julian, and Cory,
who already live in a transformed world

TABLE OF CONTENTS

FOREWORD

"The Graph"

I owe Ginger and Wayne a debt of gratitude for the use of their research during my years of advocating for two-way/dual language programs throughout California and the United States. The saying that "a picture is worth a thousand words" particularly applies to their graph showing the different programs for English learners (see page 55). It was this piece that was always the centerpiece of my presentation on dual language programs for parents, teachers, administrators and others who were interested in beginning a new two-way dual language program or those who were striving to enrich their existing dual language program.

"The Graph" was of particular importance for me as it demonstrates the actual long-term effect of dual language programs—English learners will not perform at grade level by second or third grade, but actually out-perform their peers in monolingual English programs in the later grades. As I once told a newspaper reporter, I would much prefer that my child be at grade level in eighth grade and in high school than in second grade!

One of my most vivid recollections of presenting the research using "The Graph" was with a group of parents at a school where their two-way dual language program was in danger of being eliminated. The program was young—just going into second grade and the parents were very much invested in the program. It was "The Graph" that gave the parents the knowledge base to advocate for their program. Dads, moms, older siblings ... all now had the confidence to meet with the site and school district administrators to keep their program intact.

Thank you Ginger and Wayne—your research has been invaluable to the dual language community!

Marcia Vargas
Director (Retired), Two-Way CABE
California Association for Bilingual Education

ACKNOWLEDGMENTS

The Dual Language Education of New Mexico staff have been incredibly valuable collaborators with us in producing this book. In staff meetings, they read and discussed each chapter of the book and made many suggestions based on their extensive professional experience as well as knowledge of our work. We are extremely grateful to Dee McMann, DLeNM publications editor, for her practiced eye in every detail of manuscript preparation, including rewriting occasional passages to clarify the text. We extend our deep gratitude to David Rogers, DLeNM executive director, for taking the leap to make this their first full book publication. Michael García and David Rogers spent countless hours reviewing our figures (generated over many years and varied software applications) for clarity and consistency. Other DLeNM staff—Lisa Meyer, Lorenzo Sánchez, and Dair Obenshain —made substantial contributions to strengthening the messages throughout this book.

We also owe our Deans, Gus Mellander (panameño extraordinario) and Martin Ford (the win-win master), enormous gratitude for providing us with professional support at George Mason University. They enabled us to conduct our national research studies that have substantially influenced school policies around the world over the past two decades.

To our families, we are ever so grateful for their sharing the journey with us and supporting our joint mission. And finally, cheers to our special friends in central Virginia—you know who you are—you continue to provide inspiration that helps us visualize and co-create a swiftly transforming world.

INTRODUCTION

If you make decisions about the education of one or more students acquiring a second language in school, this book was written for you. Such decisions are routinely made by teachers, parents, counselors, principals, central office administrators, and superintendents of public and private schools. In addition, this book's intended audience includes university faculty, school boards, and other state and national policy makers who influence and shape policies that affect English learners.

The information, findings, analyses, and insights in this book result from our 25 years of rewarding but sometimes arduous work with education practitioners in U.S. schools. Both they and we have learned a great deal together about what really works for English learners. We have always encouraged educators to analyze their own local school district data as a means of validating our nation-wide findings in the only terms that really matter to local stakeholders. Over the years we have been truly rewarded by the opportunities to assist many school districts in analyzing their own data. We have also encouraged other researchers to engage in the collection and analysis of large-scale, long-term data on program effectiveness for linguistically diverse students, especially English learners, and for native English speakers. As we celebrate our 25 years of collaboration, we offer this book (and the ones to follow) as a compilation of our own best work and of the best insights and interpretations from our many professional colleagues in the schools over the years.

Our overarching goal has always been social justice, in the form of equal educational opportunities for all linguistically diverse students. In the transformed world of the 21st century, all of us will benefit from improved quality of life with the final attainment of this goal. So, our heartfelt thanks go to all of you who want the best for all students, especially second language learners, and who are looking for validated education practices to achieve equal educational opportunity. This book is indeed for you.

Ginger and Wayne

EDUCATING ENGLISH LEARNERS FOR A TRANSFORMED WORLD

Virginia P. Collier and Wayne P. Thomas

DUAL LANGUAGE EDUCATION OF NEW MEXICO

ALBUQUERQUE, NM   FUENTE PRESS   FUENTE PRESS

REFLECTIONS FROM THE FIELD

The longitudinal cross-national research studies conducted by Thomas and Collier over the past few decades have provided indispensable empirical evidence in support of dual language education. For educators, researchers, and professional developers like me, Thomas and Collier's research findings are particularly relevant and vital as a foundation for further research as well as for firmly establishing dual language education as an effective, viable, and desirable alternative to subtractive and monolingual education. Their findings are an integral part of my professional development presentations to teachers, administrators, and parents alike. I find that educators and parents new to dual language education are often uneasy and skeptical about potential negative academic and linguistic results from having students participate in a program that is not fully delivered in English. The concerns tend to come mostly from parents and educators of English language learners fearing that these students will not perform well on standardized English tests. My own experiences as a dual language educator and researcher are consistently affirmed by the findings of the Thomas and Collier studies which in turn give weight and credence to my own research findings and claims about the value and effectiveness of dual language instruction.

DR. SONIA SOLTERO
DEPAUL UNIVERSITY
CHICAGO, ILLINOIS

CHAPTER ONE: TRANSFORMING U.S. SCHOOLS

Throughout the 20th and early 21st centuries, as U.S. schools have gradually developed to serve more and more students, we educators have experienced enormous swings back and forth in the educational philosophy that drives school decisions. Originally, our public schools focused on memorization and rote work to produce graduates prepared to serve the industrial revolution—factory workers who could handle long hours in assembly line production. At the same time, John Dewey's philosophies in the early 20th century encouraged a very different type of learning that focused on the flowering of the child through discovery learning. In the first decade of the 21st century, we are still struggling with these major differences in perspective. Do we do endless "drill and kill" exercises to meet the latest requirements of the tests developed under *No Child Left Behind* legislation? Or do we educate the whole child, stimulating the natural developmental learning processes with which each student is gifted? Or is there a better way to merge these two perspectives? This is the 21st century educator's dilemma.

For what is happening right now on the immediate horizon and beyond is a vast and constantly changing acceleration of life's lessons and learning in every dimension imaginable. It seems impossible to keep up with the transformations taking place in our institutions. Every field is ripe with dramatic knowledge-building. The way the world works today will not be the way it works in the next decade. So how do we keep up? For what do we educators need to prepare our students, as the next generation of leaders and service-providers? Our goal is to prepare them for their future, not for what exists now, although there are always lessons to be learned from the way things worked in the past that are included in any good educational system.

As we face our continuously transforming world, we can develop visions of our future schools—visions which may become reality in a relatively short time, because everything is accelerating these days. The Founding Fathers and Mothers of our country planted the vision in our minds that all humans are created equal. We are continuing to define what that might mean—initially, persons of color and females were left out of the picture—and we are still in the process of resolving our commitment to that ideal. But we have expanded the concept now to include the belief that all humans should receive fair treatment and equal protection under the law. In school, that means that every student arriving at our door must be treated fairly and given the same opportunities that other students receive, so that each student reaches his/her full potential. How can we do this, given the wild and wonderful range of needs and experiences that our students bring to our schools, from Bantu refugees from Somalia who have never lived inside a building and don't know what a doorknob is used for, to students who have attended schools in their country that are far in advance of our curriculum in the U.S.?

Yes, we can transform our schools, even given the vast range of students' needs. Yes, we are obligated to serve every student in meaningful ways. In fact, a U.S. Supreme Court decision requires that for English learners (*Lau v. Nichols*, 1974). Your school district may be just getting started thinking about the issues for students whose first language is not English, with new arrivals moving into your community fairly recently. Or yours may be a school district that has been working on meaningful ways of schooling English learners for over five decades. One thing is certain—things will never stay the same. Just when you think you've developed a great program that is meeting all students' needs, new arrivals with different needs appear on your school's doorstep.

But this is a time to be creative. New visions can lead to new excitement and empowerment among teachers and administrators. So let's examine the current effectiveness of U.S. schools and combine that with what the research tells us about what works with linguistically diverse students. And then we can take that foundation—research and current practice—and visualize new possibilities that build on the old, but that also reach for the future. Our students deserve nothing less.

We currently see practices evolving in the field of bilingual and English-as-a-second-language (ESL) education. The evolution is subtle but profound. More and more schools are training all teachers to include second language teaching strategies such as scaffolding and sheltered instruction techniques in their teaching practice. Many of these strategies help teachers to develop conceptual understanding for all students in more meaningful ways. Separate ESL classes for part of the school day are very helpful to students for the first year of exposure to the English language, but increasingly we are finding ways to integrate English learners into the larger student body with each succeeding year.

One of the most dramatic, evolving practices is the type of support provided in students' primary language. In the first decades of bilingual schooling in the U.S., most states with state-funded programs chose to implement transitional bilingual classes. This program model was designed to support students for 1 or 2 years with literacy development and some content area classes in their primary language while acquiring basic skills in English. The ultimate goal was to move students into the English mainstream within 2 years.

Now, many of these experienced schools are beginning to develop dual language enrichment models. In response to research showing that 1 to 2 years is inadequate for students to reach grade level in their second language, these models provide extended time for development of the two languages through the curriculum and include other groups of students who choose to be schooled through two languages.

The mix of students has led to new and more creative ways of teaching. With the demographic shifts described in the next pages, more students having completed dual language schooling at the elementary school, and the requests of English-speaking and Spanish-speaking parents who place their children in the bilingual classes, many of these programs have extended into all grades, PK–12. Thus, across the U.S. as more dual language programs have been developed, the creativity in teaching and the number of students being reached by this program model have expanded exponentially. Two states, New Mexico and Texas, have explicit state legislation encouraging this model of schooling with state guidelines for implementation, and the federal government has adopted the curricular and administrative standards developed by Dual Language Education of New Mexico *(www.dlenm. org)* as federal standards for dual language schooling.

This book is designed for all educators to study and reflect on the best ways to serve English learners. Through this process, you will discover that what works for English learners also serves all students. Best practices for English learners lead to high performing schools. This is a win-win scenario! In the remainder of this chapter, we will examine who English learners are, as well as the larger population of all linguistically diverse students, some of whom are proficient in English.

Demographics

Students whose first language is not English are the fastest-growing demographic group in public schools in all regions of the United States. The U.S. Census predicts that these students, some fluent English speakers and others not yet proficient in English, will make up 40% of the school-age population by the 2030s (Berliner & Biddle, 1995). Statistics on numbers of students working on developing English proficiency include the following for Grades K–12 across the nation's public schools: in 1990 one in 20 students were English learners; in 2008 one in nine; and U.S. demographers estimate one in four by the 2030s (Goldenberg, 2008). While our nation's 5.1 million English learners in the U.S. come from all regions of the world and speak many different languages, in 2009, 75% are of Spanish-speaking background, and 65% are born in the U.S. (*Editorial Projects in Education Research Center*, 2009, pp. 7, 12, 15).

At present, most U.S. schools are dramatically under-educating this group. Nationwide, the achievement gap between average native English speakers and students who started school with little proficiency in English is very large. By the end of high school, this achievement gap is equivalent to about 1.2 national standard deviations, as measured by standardized achievement tests across the curriculum. This represents the difference between average scores at the 50th national percentile for native English speakers and the 10th–12th percentiles for students who

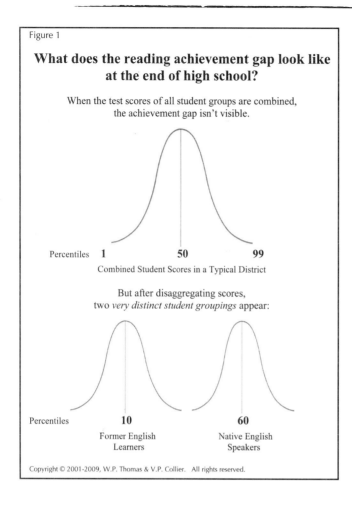

were initially classified as English learners (Thomas & Collier, 1997, 2002; see Figure 1).

In the U.S., current and former English learners with unmet needs are no longer a small minority. As a nation, we cannot afford continuation of current education practices that have produced this large gap, at the risk of under-preparing a large segment of our citizenry for the 21st century. This book provides urgently needed information for policy makers, teachers, administrators, school boards, and communities to improve the effectiveness of all school programs for these students. The good news is that many of the effective instructional strategies for English learners are also equally effective for all students. In this book, designed for staff development training and university courses, we shall examine the extensive research knowledge base that informs school effectiveness for current and former English learners, with a focus on practical decisions for educators.

Who are linguistically diverse students?

In school databases, current and former English learners are largely represented in three major federal ethnic group categories–Hispanic, Asian and Pacific Islander, and Native American. In addition to these groups, immigrants also arrive from Europe, Africa, and the Middle East. The federal government refers to all of these students as *language minorities*, a term taken from the field of sociolinguistics. *Language **majority*** students in the U.S. grow up in a home where the majority language, English, is the main or only language spoken. In contrast, *language **minority*** students of the U.S. come from a home where a language other than English is spoken (perhaps only by grandparents, but the heritage language is still an important part of the students' lives). They may include recently arriving immigrants as well as eighth-generation citizens of the U.S.

Many people feel that the commonly used term language minority can be misunderstood, especially when in some school systems they are the majority. The term minority can also carry a negative connotation, incorrectly associated with lesser social status. A less offensive term—culturally and linguistically diverse students—is preferred by many. For this book, we shall use the term *linguistically diverse* to refer to all first- and second-generation immigrants as well as ethnolinguistic groups living within U.S. boundaries that have preserved the heritage of their ancestors across many generations.

Linguistically diverse students born in the U.S. or arriving at a very young age usually experience initial cognitive and linguistic development in their family's home language and may be introduced to English for the first time when they begin schooling. If they are immigrants, they typically begin acquisition of English (their second or sometimes third language) in U.S. schools at their age of arrival in the U.S. Others may be raised in a bilingual/bicultural context from birth and can be very proficient in both English and their home language when they arrive at school, while still others may be English dominant, having lost much of their heritage language. All of these students can have unmet educational needs which are addressed by this book.

English learners

The large majority of linguistically diverse students in the U.S. start their schooling as English learners, not yet proficient in the English language. Thus we will spend a large portion of this book focused on the needs of these students who initially are classified as English learners when they enroll in U.S. schools. In federal government terminology, English learners are labeled *limited-English-proficient* (LEP) students. Since this term is considered very offensive by many students and their parents, we prefer the term widely used in the field, *English language learners*, and we use the shorter form *English learners*. Most linguistically diverse students are studying English as a second language (ESL) or have studied it sometime in their past. Thus we refer to these students as English learners (those still receiving a special program to assist them) and former English learners (those who have received services and have passed the assessment measures to be classified as English-proficient).

Staff perceptions of English learners

Some educators consider linguistically diverse students–especially those who do not yet know English–to be a big problem that they wish would somehow go away. Others consider them special resources for our country, available to add proficient bilinguals and multilinguals to the workforce, which U.S. business executives say we desperately need for participation in the global economy, and to become fully prepared replacements for the soon-to-retire baby boomers, who outnumber the succeeding generations. Thus immigrants and linguistically diverse groups will play an increasingly important role in our national productivity in the next several decades. If school districts fail to respond to these students' current unmet needs, we will live in an increasingly under-educated and under-productive society, and there may be a dire shortage of skilled workers to fill jobs of importance to the U.S. And yet, of equal or greater importance is fulfilling our country's commitment to ensuring equitable access to a quality education and educating all of our youth to the very best of our ability. In so doing, we hope to educate citizens who possess the competence and attitudes to be successful, contributing members of a thriving and diverse nation. These students are key to our future as a country, and meeting their educational needs is a matter of national importance. We educators can create a meaningful and motivating academic environment in which all students can succeed, but to do that we need to change what exists now. That's what this book is all about.

Overview of the book

Throughout this book, we are guiding educators through a process. We are asking you to reflect on the services that you have designed to serve all linguistically diverse students, including those who are not yet proficient in English. At the end of each chapter, we provide a reflection section that helps you to evaluate your current school programs.

Chapter Two provides a brief overview of federal and state policies regarding linguistically diverse students that educators need to know, including major Supreme Court decisions, federal and state legislation, and voters' referenda passed in California, Arizona, and Massachusetts. Chapter Three presents the research on how long it takes to reach grade level achievement in a second language, and Chapter Four explains why that takes so long. In Chapter Five, we examine the research on school program effectiveness, analyzing the many types of special programs designed for English learners in the U.S. and their long-term success in helping students reach grade-level achievement in English. Chapter Six expands the discussion of programs, contrasting characteristics of the highest-achieving and lowest-achieving programs for linguistically diverse students in the U.S., and discussing policy implications. Chapter Seven provides some exciting visualizations of future schools, and Chapter Eight provides action recommendations for school administrators, teachers, and education policy makers. The first two appendices provide details on several program evaluation and testing issues that are important for educators to understand.

REFLECTIONS FROM THE FIELD

AN AMERICAN INDIAN PUEBLO PERSPECTIVE

Language immersion programs in school settings are relatively recent approaches to American Indian language revitalization efforts in the United States. This is in contrast to decades-long federal government education policies that sought to eliminate Native American languages, beginning with 19th century boarding schools, well into the mid-20th century where American Indian languages have largely been ignored in public schools. Early nineteenth century federal policies, unfortunately, have resulted in long-standing legacies of many American Indian languages lost forever or nearly gone in many tribes.

DR. CHRISTINE SIMS, ACOMA PUEBLO
UNIVERSITY OF NEW MEXICO
ALBUQUERQUE, NEW MEXICO

CHAPTER TWO: THE U.S. POLICY CONTEXT

During the past four decades in the United States, the nascent and now maturing field of bilingual/ESL education experienced extensive political support in its early years, followed by periodic acerbic policy battles at federal, state, and local levels in more recent years. Too often the field has remained quite marginalized in the eyes of the education mainstream. Policy analysts suspect the rapidly growing demographics of linguistically diverse groups at the turn of the 21st century as a major underlying cause for public furor regarding providing even minimal support for English learners. Similar xenophobic fears were expressed publicly a century ago, when immigration to the U.S. was also at high levels. It is natural that those who hold the power feel that their institutions are threatened.

Nevertheless, U.S. citizens of linguistically diverse background are at least 25% of the newly entering workforce in the U.S. right now, and we need their help both to keep the economy going and to continue the contributions from immigrant groups that have enriched and strengthened our country for centuries. Hispanic and American Indian ethnolinguistic groups have a long history of belonging to this land with stable communities that strive to educate their children in a bilingual/bicultural context. Immigrants arriving from Europe and other regions of the world have also continued to shape the flourishing of this country. Past immigrants have provided a constant stimulus for new ideas as well as strong commitment to the ideals upon which the U.S. is founded. Recently arrived immigrants have demonstrated the persistent hope that they can succeed in a new life here, and they want to take responsibility for their own lives. They are great risk takers to leave their homes and start life over in a new land, and their demonstrated problem-solving skills are much needed in our society. Recognizing the potential of these groups, some school administrators in the U.S. have taken the steps to create innovative school programs that (1) accelerate the academic achievement of students whose first language is not English, and (2) enable them to fully close the achievement gap with native-English-speaking students. These educators have understood that in the long term, we all will benefit from these effective programs. In the chapters that follow, we will describe these programs and instructional approaches.

To understand educators' responsibilities for compliance with federal and state legislation and court decisions, this chapter provides an overview of major U.S. policies that apply to educating linguistically diverse students. These policies set the context for the historical development of the school programs that now exist to serve the needs of English learners. They also define the rights of linguistically diverse students as well as establishing guidelines for providing them with an appropriate education.

Court decisions

Basic rights. The basic rights of linguistically diverse students are based on three major foundations in U.S. law. First, the U.S. Supreme Court's interpretation of the 14th Amendment of the U.S. Constitution guarantees all persons equal protection under the laws of the United States. Second, Title VI of the Civil Rights Act of 1964 bans discrimination on the basis of race, color, or national origin in any federally assisted program. Third, the Equal Educational Opportunities Act of 1974 requires that all public school districts must "take appropriate action to overcome language barriers that impede equal participation by its students in its instructional programs" (Ovando, Combs & Collier, 2006, p. 74). All U.S. court decisions focused on the educational needs of linguistically diverse students who are English learners have been based on and have extended the interpretations of these basic rights.

Hernández v. Texas (1954). This legal decision was a landmark U.S. Supreme Court case, ruling that Mexican Americans and all other ethnic groups in the United States have equal protection under the 14th Amendment of the U.S. Constitution. Since the 14th Amendment explicitly focuses on equal protection for whites and blacks, this case extended these rights to other ethnic minorities in this ruling.

Lau v. Nichols (1974). The landmark U.S. Supreme Court decision, *Lau v. Nichols* continues to be the most significant federal court decision defining legal responsibilities of schools serving English learners. The key issue in this important ruling is defined as providing a *meaningful education.* Just teaching the mainstream curriculum in English is not considered meaningful.

> *There is no equality of treatment merely by providing students with the same facilities, textbooks, teachers, and curriculum; for students who do not understand English are effectively foreclosed from any meaningful education.*
>
> *Basic English skills are at the very core of what these public schools teach. Imposition of a requirement that, before a child can effectively participate in the education program, he must already have acquired those basic skills is to make a mockery of public education. We know that those who do not understand English are certain to find their classroom experiences wholly incomprehensible and in no way meaningful.*

Supreme Court Justice William O. Douglas, *Lau v. Nichols,* 1974

This particular lawsuit was filed by the Chinese-American community in San Francisco, and in this case the negotiated consensus agreement required that bilingual schooling be provided to keep students academically on grade level while learning English. But the key words *a meaningful education* may be interpreted differently in other educational contexts. In other words, *Lau v. Nichols* does not explicitly require bilingual schooling, but it does mean that school districts must provide some kind of support program for English learners that enables them to have a meaningful education.

Castañeda v. Pickard (1981). Extending the interpretation of what a meaningful education might be for English learners, the next most significant court decision affecting linguistically diverse students was *Castañeda v. Pickard*. This federal Fifth Circuit Court of Appeals decision in Texas has been used as a standard for all succeeding court cases as well as for Office for Civil Rights guidelines for compliance with the *Lau v. Nichols* Supreme Court decision. The *Castañeda* ruling formulated three criteria for evaluating programs serving English learners. The program must be (1) based on sound educational theory recognized by experts in the field; (2) implemented effectively, with adequate resources and personnel; and (3) evaluated and found effective in both the teaching of languages (English and students' first language if the program is bilingual) and in access to the full curriculum (math, social studies, science). As we review program effectiveness research in the next chapters, we will be applying these evaluation criteria.

Plyler v. Doe (1982). One more landmark U.S. Supreme Court case should be mentioned here. *Plyler v. Doe* guarantees the rights of undocumented immigrants to free public education. Public schools are prohibited from (1) denying undocumented students admission to school, (2) requiring students or parents to disclose or document their immigration status, or (3) requiring social security numbers of all students (Carrera, 1989).

Federal legislation

In this accountability era, with the passage of the federal *No Child Left Behind Act* of 2001, the major impact of this legislation on local schools serving linguistically diverse students is the new requirement that achievement data be disaggregated by groups, including ethnic groups and English learners, with the goal of closing the achievement gap between groups over the next decade. (We will make research-based recommendations for how this can be done in the two appendices of this book.) Federal stimulus funding has been provided to the states to improve programs for linguistically diverse students under Title III of the *No Child Left Behind Act* (NCLB), but many states have not yet provided the leadership to use this funding for local school programs based on the research knowledge base in the field. Disaggregation of test scores has led to recognizing unmet group needs, but the NCLB-required cross-sectional comparisons (comparing different students—such as fourth graders last year to fourth graders this year) are inappropriate. Only longitudinal comparisons (following the same students across time) appropriately measure student achievement.

There are at least three major changes that the next version of NCLB (referred to here as NCLB Version 2.0) should include (see Figure 2). First, longitudinal comparisons—following the same students across time—are much more valid for measuring student achievement than the presently required cross-sectional comparisons—comparing student groups from last year to a different group of this year's students in the same grade. This is especially true in high stakes situations. Second, there is conclusive research support for the position that "3 years is not enough" for typical English learners to completely close their achievement gap with native English speakers. In fact, 3 years is enough to close only about half of the full gap. Thus, if full gap closure is really the goal of NCLB, then the federal funding for English learner programs should be extended from the present 3 years (a politically convenient figure lacking research justification) to at least 6 years. This would allow enough time for an effective program to fully close the gap for typical English learners.

Third, English learners should be tested in their primary language for high stakes or accountability purposes until their mastery of the testing language (English) is equivalent to that of their native English-speaking peers. Recent empirical research shows that English learners acquire enough English proficiency to be tested equitably in English only after 5 to 6 years of schooling (Tsang, Katz & Stack,

---

Figure 2

No Child Left Behind (NCLB) Requires:

✓ **Achievement gap closure**, rather than group gains as the measure of success

✓ **Disaggregation of test scores by student groups** with Adequate Yearly Progress (AYP) required for all groups

HOWEVER, NCLB also inappropriately requires high-stakes accountability decisions using potentially flawed data by cross-sectionally comparing the achievement of different groups of students in successive years.

NCLB – Version 2.0 (As *Revised*) Should Include:

✓ **Longitudinal (same students in successive years) rather than cross-sectional** achievement comparisons by classes, schools, and districts

✓ **Adequate funding for a minimum of 6 years of student support,** based on scientific research findings. Research shows that **3 years is not enough** for typical English learners to fully close the achievement gap!

✓ A provision allowing **accountability testing in students' primary language** while they're acquiring English, followed by testing in English after full achievement gap closure is attained in 5–8 years

---

2008). School districts that test English learners in English after 1 to 3 years (before they have fully acquired English to native-speaking standards) artificially lower their English learners' content achievement test scores, leading to falsely low scores for accountability purposes. Their scores on the same curricular content would typically be higher if tested in their primary language for curricular mastery assessment purposes. In fact, English learners' grade-level achievement in their primary language is the most powerful predictor of eventual grade-level achievement in English (Thomas & Collier, 1997, 2002).

Beginning in 1968 with the passage of Title VII of the Elementary and Secondary Education Act, past federal legislation provided a small percentage of stimulus funds, applied for competitively, for local school districts who chose to create new programs or improve their existing programs for English learners. Subsequent reauthorizations of the legislation generally kept the funding level for these competitive grants much lower than for any other program for children with special needs, especially when compared to other federal education funds for children of poverty, migrant education, and special education.

For the last 5 years, Agua Fría Elementary School in Santa Fe, New Mexico, has had a 90:10 two-way Spanish/English Immersion Strand that has complemented the English and bilingual maintenance strands at our prekindergarten through sixth grade community school. ... The work of Virginia Collier and Wayne Thomas has allowed our school to (1) design a program, (2) support its continued growth based on our site's AYP "school in need of improvement" status, and (3) shape an informed response to NCLB. One aspect of that response has been the creation of an assessment data infrastructure to collect and analyze Spanish/English literacy assessment data. This is a new path that would not have been possible without the trailblazing work of Collier and Thomas to allow data to inform best practice dual language education program development.

SUZANNE JÁCQUEZ GORMAN, PH.D.
PRINCIPAL, AGUA FRÍA ELEMENTARY SCHOOL
SANTA FE, NEW MEXICO

While federal funding is currently influencing state policies by requiring accountability measures (assuming that states choose to accept the federal funds, and most states have chosen to participate), it must be kept in mind that the U.S. Constitution does not explicitly mention education as a duty of the federal government. Thus the ultimate responsibility for education policy decision making resides at the state level by provision of the 10th Amendment, and the states commonly delegate some control to the local levels. But federal influence also comes in the form of compliance with federal court decisions and basic rights guaranteed to residents of all states by the U.S. Constitution. These are enforced by the U.S. Office for Civil Rights, which has varied its enforcement policies depending on the political party in power. Many school districts with large numbers of linguistically diverse students are operating under agreements, negotiated with the Office for Civil Rights, that have been based on local, state, and federal court decisions for their region. These agreements usually outline minimal, rather than educationally appropriate, services that must be provided for English learners. In general, federal policies have assisted schools somewhat, but the main impetus for school improvement for linguistically diverse students has come at state and local levels.

... In the American southwest, where American Indian language maintenance programs have emerged over the last decade, one-way heritage language immersion approaches have supported American Indian students in re-learning these languages. The long-term research of renowned researchers such as Virginia Collier and Wayne Thomas has both enlightened and bolstered practitioners and teachers of American Indian languages. In several Pueblo Indian tribes of New Mexico, for example, such research has been instrumental in developing language programs that have brought renewed value to languages spoken nowhere else in the world. Their research has validated the wisdom of maintaining heritage languages rather than trying to erase them in deference to English. Furthermore, their studies have shown that students can indeed make academic gains by maintaining and developing heritage languages while at the same time developing strong academic English skills. ... tribal communities are observing that children who are afforded consistent language learning opportunities in well-developed language programs are making important strides towards becoming the next generation of American Indian language speakers.

Dr. Christine Sims
Acoma Pueblo
University of New Mexico

State legislation and voters' referenda

The history of state legislation illustrates the ups and downs of the politics of the field of bilingual/ESL education. During the first half of the 20th century, several states had statutory prohibitions against the use of languages other than English for instruction in schools. But along with the federal passage of the 1968 Bilingual Education Act, many states passed legislation to assist local school districts with implementation of bilingual and ESL services. By 1971, 30 states permitted or required some form of bilingual instruction. By 1983, bilingual education was explicitly permitted by law in 43 states, and 21 of these states provided some form of special funding for school districts to use for English learners. As of 2009, 43 states encourage or allow bilingual instruction, and seven states restrict or ban native language instruction for English learners (*Editorial Projects in Education Research Center*, 2009, p. 26). The seven states with restrictions are Arizona, Arkansas, California, Connecticut, Massachusetts, New Hampshire, and Wisconsin.

But it is important to know that there are many varied forms of bilingual and ESL schooling, a point often overlooked by the popular media. Along with varying amounts of instruction through students' first language, all forms of bilingual schooling (federal, state, and local) include English as a second language taught through academic content. Short-term remedial forms of bilingual instruction, often referred to as transitional bilingual education, are the type most frequently assumed when someone uses the term "bilingual education." But states and local school districts also support longer-term remedial bilingual programs and enrichment bilingual models. We shall examine these many variations and their varied success in helping English learners reach grade level achievement in English in Chapters Five and Six.

A few examples illustrate the large variations in states' policies and the types of bilingual and ESL programs that are state-funded. In 1969, New Mexico, an official bilingual state, was the first state to pass legislation authorizing instruction in languages other than English. New Mexico state legislation passed in 2002 is the most comprehensive state funding plan of any state in the U.S. for developing enrichment bilingual/ESL programs based on the effectiveness research in bilingual/ESL education.

In 1971, by way of contrast, Massachusetts was the first state to mandate transitional bilingual instruction, a form of bilingual schooling encouraged in the 1968 federal legislation. Transitional bilingual education is now the most common bilingual program model across the U.S. But in the November 2002 election, a majority of Massachusetts voters supported English-only program legislation. The English-only movement has also succeeded in defeating bilingual education legislation in Arizona and California through voter referenda. Proposition 227 of California, requiring English immersion classes for one year followed by the English mainstream, has been in place since 1998. Research data are now available for this program, and this will be reported on in Chapters Five and Six. In spite of Proposition 227, some schools in California have implemented two-way bilingual enrichment programs, designed for all students. To qualify, schools must request a waiver from the state requirements of the voter referendum.

The state of Texas currently has a strong bilingual education law in place, providing state funding for longer-term transitional bilingual education services for students in Grades PK–5. In addition, Texas has passed enabling state legislation to encourage the expansion of dual language education (an enrichment bilingual program) for all students, to graduate students who are proficient bilinguals for the workforce of the 21st century.

In summary, several U.S. Supreme Court and federal court decisions require that U.S. schools educate every child that walks through our schools' doors and that we must provide special support for English learners. U.S. educators are obligated to do more than simply submersing English learners in the English mainstream. The federal legislation, *No Child Left Behind*, also requires that schools test all students. This means following English learners (among others) to see that they are closing the achievement gap with time. Federal and state funding can provide support for school districts to develop quality schooling for linguistically diverse students, most of whom start school as English learners, if educators are knowledgeable regarding the research on effectiveness and prepared to use the funds creatively. The following chapters of this book summarize this research and suggest creative ways to reform U.S. schools.

Analyzing your school and school district

As a first step, begin considering these questions with stakeholders in your school community or district:

- Do you know if your state has passed state legislation regarding the education of English learners?

- Is any state funding available for your school district?

- Are there requirements in the state legislation that you must follow?

- Is your school district in compliance with all state and federal regulations regarding English learners?

- How have you analyzed the effectiveness of your current programs and practices?

- Is there federal government funding that you might apply for, in order to develop new ways of schooling English learners?

REFLECTIONS FROM THE FIELD

For 23 years, Francis Scott Key Elementary School ~ Escuela Key in Arlington, Virginia, has been a 50:50 two-way Spanish Immersion school. Since 1986, it has grown from 40 to 640 students. Between Key and Claremont there are over 1200 elementary immersion students in Arlington. Fortunately, immersion opportunities through twelfth grade allow students to perfect their language abilities before graduation.

At Key School, where every child is a second language learner and is challenged to perform in their native and target language, students thrive and excel using one another as language models. All children learn in an inclusive classroom where students with disabilities and those who are newly arrived learn and grow with gifted and regular students. They may not all meet the standards in their early years, but they do once they have had enough time in a stimulating and academically rich environment.

DR. MARJORIE L. MYERS
PRINCIPAL, KEY SCHOOL ~ ESCUELA KEY
ARLINGTON, VIRGINIA

CHAPTER THREE: HOW LONG TO FULL GAP CLOSURE?

To understand the many types of U.S. school programs that have evolved to serve the special needs of students whose first language is not English, background knowledge from the research provides an important conceptual framework. We will present this framework by identifying key decisions that educators have to make when planning or improving the services provided to English learners.

The first major decision is a thorny problem connected to school funding of these services. Remember that *Lau v. Nichols* (1974) requires some form of special services so that English learners can receive a "meaningful education." **But how long should an English learner receive special services?** If the school district has chosen a costly program, the school board and administrators will always be revisiting this issue and questioning the length of time that students stay in the program. A common rationale for shortening the program is that the sooner they can move the students into the mainstream, the less expense to the school district. But others argue that in the long term, if students are not well served in the mainstream, the greater sustained cost to the community will be large numbers of students achieving at low levels and more students prematurely leaving high school because the schools are not meeting their needs. Solutions to these dilemmas have focused on less costly but well implemented and effective special programs as well as redesigning the mainstream to serve students more effectively. We shall visit the specifics of these program changes in the course of the next several chapters.

To tackle the research addressing this "how long" question, our own research findings as well as those of many other researchers have shed much light on this complex issue. In 1985 and continuing to the present, we (the authors) began a long series of studies in large and middle-sized urban and suburban school districts as well as smaller rural school districts, addressing how long English learners take to reach grade-level achievement in a second language when they start school with no proficiency in that second language (English). In other words, when English learners are tested on grade-level school tests given in English across the curriculum–reading, writing, language arts, mathematics, science, and social studies–how long does it take them to reach the typical performance of native English speakers of their age group scoring at the 50th percentile (which defines grade-level) on the required standardized, norm-referenced or criterion-referenced tests or performance assessments. The "how long" research question can be visually conceptualized in Figure 3.1.

The left side of the figure shows what we have found to be English learners' typical performance on grade-level tests in English after they have been supported by ESL pullout classes for 2 to 3 years in the elementary school years. Their performance is quite low when they first take this type of difficult grade-level test in English, usually in the later elementary school years. As can be seen in Figure 3.1, English learners start at the 20th normal curve equivalent (NCE), which is the 8th percentile. (We will be reporting throughout this book in NCEs, which are equal-interval percentiles, appropriate measures for comparisons. But since most administrators are more familiar with percentiles, we will give the equivalent percentile each time we provide an NCE score. To understand the concepts of percentiles and normal curve equivalents, see Appendix A.) The goal is for the two test score distributions of English learners and native English speakers, initially with very different average scores, to eventually be equivalent, represented by the two overlapping 50th percentile distributions on the right side of the figure. When these two different group distributions of test scores have become indistinguishable over time, the achievement gap has been closed. The gap initially is around 30 NCEs, or expressed in percentiles, from the 8th to the 50th percentile.

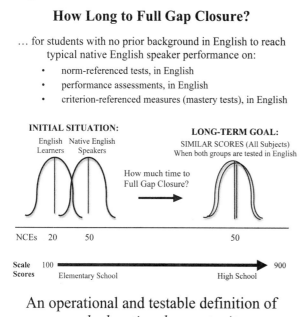

Figure 3.1

How Long to Full Gap Closure?

… for students with no prior background in English to reach typical native English speaker performance on:

- norm-referenced tests, in English
- performance assessments, in English
- criterion-referenced measures (mastery tests), in English

INITIAL SITUATION:

English Learners   Native English Speakers

LONG-TERM GOAL:
SIMILAR SCORES (All Subjects)
When both groups are tested in English

How much time to Full Gap Closure?

NCEs   20   50   50

Scale Scores   100 ———————————————▶ 900
Elementary School   High School

An operational and testable definition of *equal educational opportunity*:

The test score distributions of English learners and native English speakers are initially quite different. However, over time the English learner distribution should gradually move toward the native English speaker distribution until they are *equivalent* by the end of their school years as measured by on-grade-level tests of all school subjects administered in English.

Closing the achievement gap is the ultimate goal for the federal *No Child Left Behind* Act and for accompanying state accountability systems, so the "how long" research question provides answers to these urgent concerns for which administrators and teachers are being held accountable. To understand the formidable journey that English learners must take to reach 50th percentile performance, it is important to realize that native English speakers are not just sitting around waiting for English learners to catch up. Instead, typical native English speakers are making 10 months of progress on all school subjects every 10-month school year. That's what it takes to stay on grade level. So the English learners must make more than 1 year's progress for many years in a row to eventually catch up to the native English speakers. The process requires not only learning academic English but also catching up to grade level across all academic subjects. For example, English learners must make 15 months' progress for 6 years in a row to reach grade level achievement in second language. (See Figure 3.2.)

How long to full gap closure when U.S. schooling is only in English?

Our initial decision to pursue this line of research was based on Jim Cummins' (1981) study analyzing 1,210 immigrants who arrived in Canada at age 6 or younger and at that age were first exposed to the English language. In this study, Cummins found that when following these students across the school years, with data broken down by age on arrival and length of residence in Canada, it took at least 5 to 7 years, on the average, for them to approach grade-level norms on school tests that measure cognitive-academic language development in English. Cummins (1996, 2000) distinguishes between social (context-embedded) language and academic (context-reduced, cognitively demanding) language, stating that a significant level of fluency in social uses of second language (English) can be achieved in 2 to 3 years; whereas the type of second language used in academic schooling and testing contexts requires 5 to 7 years or more to develop to the level of a native speaker.

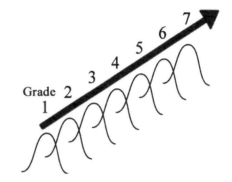

Figure 3.2

An Important Understanding

Typical native English speakers (at the 50th Percentile or NCE) make <u>one year of achievement gain during each school year</u> (10 months' gain in a 10-month school year).

Therefore: English learners must gain MORE THAN ONE YEAR'S ACHIEVEMENT (e.g., 15 months' gain per year) in each of SEVERAL CONSECUTIVE SCHOOL YEARS to ever close their typical 25 NCE achievement gap with English speakers WHEN TESTED IN ENGLISH (L2).

Since many school administrators have been extremely skeptical that 5 to 7 years are needed for the typical immigrant student to become fully proficient in academic English, with many policy makers insisting that there must be a way to speed up the process, we decided to pursue this research question for several years with varied school databases in the United States. Our initial studies, first reported in Collier (1987) and Collier & Thomas (1989), took place in a large, relatively affluent, suburban school district with a highly regarded ESL program, and a typical ESL class size of 6 to 12 students. We chose this model ESL program with the expectation that we would find that these advantaged immigrant students would be on grade level in English in a shorter time than Cummins found in his study. The student samples consisted of 1,548 and 2,014 immigrant students just beginning their acquisition of English, 65% of whom were of Asian descent and 20% of Hispanic descent, the rest representing 75 languages from around the world. These students received 1 to 3 hours per day of ESL instructional support, attending mainstream (grade-level) classes the remainder of the school day, and were generally exited from ESL within the first 2 years of their arrival in the U.S., having passed the school district's English proficiency measures for moving into the mainstream full time.

In these first studies, we limited our analyses to only those newly arriving immigrant students who were assessed when they arrived in this country as being at or above grade level in their home country schooling in native language, since we expected this "advantaged" on-grade-level group to achieve academically in their second language in the shortest time possible. It was quite a surprise to find a similar pattern to that which Cummins found, but for most groups of students it took even longer than 5 to 7 years. We found that students who arrived between ages 8 and 11, having received at least 2 to 5 years of schooling taught through their primary language in their home country, were the lucky ones who took only 5 to 7 years. Those who arrived before age 8 required an average of 7 to 10 years or more to reach grade level in English, and many never made it to grade level because they ran out of school years first.

These children arriving during the early childhood years (before age 8) had the same background characteristics as the 8- to 11-year-old arrivals. The only difference between the two groups was that the younger children had received little or no formal schooling in their first language, and this factor appeared to be a significant predictor in these first studies. **First language schooling, whether in home country or in the U.S., has now been confirmed as a key variable** in our succeeding studies on the "how long" question as well as in many other researchers' work (e.g. Baker, 2006; Baker & Prys Jones, 1998; Cummins, 1991, 1996, 2000; Díaz & Klingler, 1991; Dutcher, 2001; Freeman & Freeman, 2001, 2002; García, 1993, 1994; Genesee, 1987, 1994; Genesee, Lindholm-Leary, Saunders & Christian, 2006; Goldenberg, 2008; Greene, 1997; Hakuta, 1986; Howard & Sugarman, 2007; Lindholm-Leary, 1991, 2001; McLaughlin, 1992; Pérez & Torres-Guzmán, 2002; Ramírez, Yuen, Ramey & Pasta, 1991; Rolstad, Mahoney & Glass, 2005; Slavin & Cheung, 2003; Snow, 1990; Tabors & Snow, 2001; Tinajero & Ada, 1997; Willig, 1985; Wong Fillmore & Valadez, 1986).

In our initial studies, those arriving after age 12 with good formal schooling in their first language were making steady gains with each year of school. But by the end of high school, they had run out of time to catch up academically to the native English speakers, who were constantly pulling ahead (by making their typical 1 year's progress each year and staying on grade level). Their pattern during high school of making more gains than the native English speaker with each year of schooling would predict that they would close the gap sometime during their undergraduate schooling, if they were allowed to continue in college.

Students of all ages reached grade-level achievement in mathematics and language arts (measuring easily taught discrete points in the English language) in a shorter period of time, but they required many years to reach grade level in reading, science, and social studies in English. The measures that we use to analyze student achievement are standardized, on-grade-level, norm-referenced and criterion-referenced tests given in English across the curriculum. These are the ultimate measures of attainment for eventual competition with native English speakers on the standardized tests required for admission to a 4-year university. These tests are inappropriate measures in the first 2 to 3 years of English learners' schooling in their second language. When administered in English, the tests underestimate what these students actually know and can demonstrate when tested in their first language, and the second language tests should not be used yet for purposes of high-stakes assessment (Tsang, Katz & Stack, 2008). After 3 years, only about one half of the gap will be closed in the second language, and academic tests in students' primary language yield the most valid scores, if such tests are available. But eventually these school tests in English across the curriculum become more appropriate measures to examine. These tests help parents and educators to know whether their children will eventually gain access to the same educational opportunities that native English speakers have, by achieving educational parity (closing the achievement gap) with native English speakers while in school.

The insights gained from our initial studies led us to pursue the question with additional databases as well as research syntheses on other researchers' work on the "how long" question (Collier, 1987, 1988, 1989, 1992, 1995b, 1995c; Collier & Thomas, 1989, 2004, 2005, 2007; Collier, Thomas & Tinajero, 2006; Thomas, 1992; Thomas & Collier, 1997, 2002; Thomas, Collier & Abbott, 1993). We have now conducted studies in U.S. public schools in 35 school districts and 16 states, from 1985 to the present, analyzing over 6.2 million student records. (A student record is all available information on one student in 1 school year.) In all of our data analyses, as well as other researchers' work, we have continued to find the same general pattern when English learners are schooled all in English and tested in English. Among the most advantaged immigrant students who have had at least 4 years of on-grade-level schooling in their primary language in their home country before they arrive in the U.S., the shortest period of time for typical English learners to match the achievement of typical native English speakers is 5 years. In contrast, many English learners schooled only in English, with no home country or home language schooling, do not ever reach the same levels of achievement as typical native English speakers.

Furthermore, we have found that students being schooled all in English initially make dramatic gains in the early grades, whatever type of program they receive, and this misleads teachers and administrators into assuming that the students are going to continue to do extremely well after their special services end. But of course their school work gets more cognitively complex with each succeeding grade level. After being exited from ESL support, with each additional year in the mainstream, these students tend to fall behind the typical achievement levels of native English speakers (defined as the 50th percentile or NCE) by 1–4 NCEs each year, resulting in a very significant, cumulative achievement gap of 15–26 NCEs by the end of their school years.

It is important to understand that typical English learners in all program groups achieve significant gains each year, as do typical native English speakers. But when comparing groups, English learners who have received all their schooling exclusively through English might achieve 6 to 8 months' gain each school year as they reach the middle and high school years, less than the 10-month gain of typical native English speakers. Thus, an achievement gap with native English speakers that was partially closed in elementary school becomes wider with each passing year after elementary school, as typical native English speakers continue to advance by making 10 months' gain in 10 months' time to maintain their average score at the 50th NCE across the years.

In our 2002 national study (Thomas & Collier, 2002), we found that after English learners are exited from the special program designed to assist them during the years they are acquiring proficiency in English, they typically make less than one year's progress for each year in the mainstream. In other words, gap closure ceases after English learners leave their special programs. Yet they need to make more than one year's gain every year for several years in a row to eventually close the achievement gap with native English speakers that was only partially closed while they received special services. Instead they maintain or widen the gap in the mainstream. But when English learners participate in more effective enrichment models such as dual language education, rather than isolated, remedial models, they continue to accelerate their growth with more than one year's progress each year, leading to full achievement gap closure and long-term success in English. We will introduce these types of programs in Chapter Five.

How long to full gap closure when U.S. schooling is in the students' primary language and English?

After continuing to hear the insistent voice of policy makers to find a way to "speed up" or accelerate the process, we began to examine the progress of students in bilingual programs. Could the process of bilingual schooling speed up the acquisition of academic English and academic achievement in general?

What we found again was quite a surprise. We limited our analyses to students attending well-implemented bilingual classes taught by experienced bilingual teachers, and we used as a measure of consistency the students' level of academic achievement in their first language. Those students on grade level in their first language (i.e., tested in curricular subjects) reached on-grade-level performance in English, their second language, in all subject areas in 4 to 7 years.

At first these data analyses appeared to present a rather bleak picture–that it takes a long, long time whatever the program–until we examined the long-term picture for Grades K–12 with additional data from five large, experienced school districts. What we found is that following these students throughout their schooling, **the bilingually-schooled students were able to sustain the gains in English**, and in some cases, to achieve even higher than typical native-English-speaker performance as they moved through the secondary years of school. In other words, once bilingually-schooled students "get there" (where "there" is parity with comparable native English speakers of similar age on the school tests in English), they stay there, achieving on or above grade level in their second language. In contrast, English learners schooled only in English do not sustain the gains they made during the elementary school years when compared to typical native-English-speaker gains across the years.

Figure 3.3 illustrates the pattern of gap closure for English learners attending a dual language enrichment program, which is the program with the highest success rate in the shortest amount of time. By making more than a year's progress every year in English (amounting to a 15-month gain while the native English speakers are making a 10-month gain in their native language), they catch up to grade-level achievement in their second language after 6 years of school. The stimulus for this dramatic cognitive growth is at least a half day of grade-level schooling through their primary language.

Summary of "how long" findings for English learners

So it takes typical bilingually-schooled students, who are achieving on grade level in their first language, from 4 to 7 years to make it to the 50th NCE in their second language. It takes typical "advantaged" immigrants with 4 to 5 years of on-grade-level home country schooling in their first language from 5 to 7 years to reach the

Closing the Achievement Gap
Dual Language: The Best Case—Testing in English

Year Of School	Native English Speakers		English Language Learners	
	Growth In English Reading Achievement Across the Curriculum	Average Test Score (NCEs)	Growth In English Reading Achievement Across the Curriculum	Average Test Score (NCEs)
Start		50		20
End of Grade 1	1 year of growth	50	1 year of growth + 5 NCEs	25
End of Grade 2	1 year of growth	50	1 year of growth + 5 NCEs	30
End of Grade 3	1 year of growth	50	1 year of growth + 5 NCEs	35
End of Grade 4	1 year of growth	50	1 year of growth + 5 NCEs	40
End of Grade 5	1 year of growth	50	1 year of growth + 5 NCEs	45
End of Grade 6	1 year of growth	50	1 year of growth + 5 NCEs	50
Totals	After 6 years of growth	50	After 6 years of growth + 30 NCEs	50

Normal Curve Equivalents (NCEs) are equal-sized national percentiles.

50th NCE in their second language, when schooled all in English in the U.S. The majority of young immigrants schooled all in English in the U.S. do not make it to the 50th NCE. Those who do receive ESL through academic content for 3 to 4 years typically reach the 34th NCE (23rd percentile) by the end of high school. The minority that do make it to the 50th NCE require a minimum of 7 to 10 years, with some support for first language academic and cognitive development at home.

How long for native English speakers to reach grade-level in second language?

Since it is a common assumption among school policy makers that it should not take such a long time, one might wonder if these generalizations apply only to immigrant students. To answer that question, we examined the longitudinal achievement of native English speakers whose parents chose to have their children placed in a two-way bilingual class. These students include those with many advantages. For example, their first language, English, is not threatened in any way. English is the status and power language of the U.S., as well as of the world. They get nonstop support for their English development in school and in the larger community. We have examined English-speaking Euro-American children of middle and lower income homes, as well as African American children of middle and lower income homes who have chosen to attend bilingual classes. The middle-income children often have parents cheering them on, providing first language cognitive and academic support at home.

How long does it take these "advantaged" English speakers to reach grade-level in their second language? Figure 3.4 illustrates how native English speakers experience the same pattern as that of English learners, when they are schooled bilingually. The typical time frame for these students to reach the point where they can show off what they know on the school tests in their second language, at the level of a native speaker of that language, is 4 to 7 years. These middle-income students achieve on or above grade level in English, their first language, with each year of school. But it still takes until at least fourth or fifth grade for the typical students in this group to make it to the 50th NCE on school tests in their second language. Once they get there, they stay there and can demonstrate what they know in either their first or second language, as long as second language grade-level academic work continues to be provided in the bilingual class. Since these "advantaged" English speakers require 4 to 7 years to reach full academic proficiency in their second language, we should not be surprised when English learners take this long (or longer) to become fully proficient in *their* second language. In other researchers' studies, in the U.S. as well as other countries, similar results have been found around the world when following bilingually schooled students long-term (Baker & Prys Jones, 1998; Cazabon, Nicoladis & Lambert, 1998; Collier, 1992; Cummins, 2000; de Jong, 2002; Genesee, 1987; Howard & Sugarman, 2007; Lindholm-Leary, 1990, 2001; Lindholm-Leary & Aclan, 1991; Thomas & Collier, 1997, 2002).

Figure 3.4

Closing the Achievement Gap
Dual Language: The Best Case – Testing in Spanish

Year Of School	Native Spanish Speakers		Native English Speakers	
	Growth In Spanish Reading Achievement Across the Curriculum	Average Test Score (NCEs)	Growth In Spanish Reading Achievement Across the Curriculum	Average Test Score (NCEs)
Start		50		20
End of Grade 1	1 year of growth	50	1 year of growth + 5 NCEs	25
End of Grade 2	1 year of growth	50	1 year of growth + 5 NCEs	30
End of Grade 3	1 year of growth	50	1 year of growth + 5 NCEs	35
End of Grade 4	1 year of growth	50	1 year of growth + 5 NCEs	40
End of Grade 5	1 year of growth	50	1 year of growth + 5 NCEs	45
End of Grade 6	1 year of growth	50	1 year of growth + 5 NCEs	50
Totals	After 6 years of growth	50	After 6 years of growth + 30 NCEs	50

Normal Curve Equivalents (NCEs) are equal-sized national percentiles.

In summary, this notion that it should take students just a short time to acquire English as a second language for academic purposes and reach grade level achievement in English is clearly not supported by the research findings. Most of the programs for English learners funded by federal and state monies have used an arbitrary limit of 3 years. This amount of time was purely a guess on policy makers' part, but it has become institutionalized in both federal and state policies with no research support. Even worse for English learners, the English-only movement has pushed schools to provide only one year of ESL support! It is absurd to expect students to acquire English for schooling in only one year. This point is very well supported by linguistics research, as well as education and social science research. Policy makers who assume that minimal programs will fully close the achievement gap are risking the substantial penalties of the *No Child Left Behind* legislation. But more importantly, they are knowingly risking the future well-being of English learners participating in these minimal programs. In the next chapter, we shall examine the ongoing developmental processes that accompany linguistic development. School programs that provide nonstop support for these processes are the key to all students' academic success.

Analyzing your school and school district

Next steps to take: Conduct a needs assessment in your school and school district. There is nothing like analyzing your own school district's data to answer the questions that you have, including this "how long" question. The federal and state assessment systems as of mid-year 2009 are based on comparing, for example, last year's third graders to this year's third graders. But this is completely inappropriate, comparing two different groups of students that may have very different background characteristics and needs. Still, your school board wants to know how your students are really doing.

We recommend the *Thomas-Collier test*—a relatively quick analysis of your test scores that is more valid and reliable. (See Appendix B.) The key is to disaggregate your data by groups. The simplest break-down of your data can be focused on three groups: former English learners, linguistically diverse students who were never classified as English learners, and native English speakers. Examine data for the highest grade level tested at your school—for example, fifth graders in elementary school, eighth graders in middle school, eleventh graders in high school. Choose for the analyses only those students who have been in your school system at least 5 to 6 years, because we find that's the shortest time it typically takes to close the academic achievement gap when students are tested in English. We use the term "former" English learners, because you're looking for those who started kindergarten or first grade with beginning levels of English but by fifth grade most of these English learners have been reclassified as "fluent" English speakers. Your main goal is to see how these students who were English learners when they entered your schools are doing after 5 to 6 years of schooling in your school district.

We have yet to find one school district that has successfully fully closed the achievement gap for all their former English learners—so this goal is quite challenging. In these analyses, we also often find a smaller but significant gap between the linguistically diverse students who never received special bilingual/ESL services and the native English speakers. Both of these groups can benefit from a reconceived school program. If there are other at-risk groups attending your school district, we recommend that you disaggregate your data further. Any students not reaching grade-level achievement have the same challenges that English learners experience—having to make more than one year's progress every year to eventually catch up to the constantly advancing native-English-speaking students who stay on grade level year after year (the "norm" group). This is what this book is all about—we're guiding you to visualize new ways of schooling all students together so that everyone benefits.

REFLECTIONS FROM THE FIELD

Educators must take great care not to buy into the myth of poverty as an excuse for low academic achievement—that students of poverty cannot achieve because they do not have access to books, they lack structure in the home, or worse yet, their parents don't value education. Yes, research has shown there is a link, but that does not absolve us of our responsibility to design and implement programs that help us overcome such challenges.

When you think about it, our students are not poor during the 7 hours a day that they are in our schools. They are well fed, have access to books, are surrounded by caring adults who provide structure and who value education. We must ask, "What are our expectations for ourselves and our students during the 7 hours a day in which they are not poor?"

EDWARD TABET-CUBERO,
PRINCIPAL, WASHINGTON ELEMENTARY
WOODBURN, OREGON

CHAPTER FOUR: UNDERSTANDING THE "HOW LONG" QUESTION: THE PRISM MODEL

Why does it take so long? Why do so many students schooled only in second language fail to reach the 50th percentile on norm-referenced tests? Why do so few English learners reach the typical performance of the native English speaker on criterion-referenced tests, even when they are given intensive coursework all in English? Why does it take typical bilingually-schooled students a minimum of 4 years, and as long as 7 years, to "show what they know" in their second language at performance levels typical of native speakers?

To help policy makers understand the complex process of second language acquisition within a school context, we have developed a conceptual model that has emerged from our research findings, as well as from other researchers' work. The research syntheses upon which the Prism Model is based, from research in education, linguistics, and the social sciences, can be found in Collier (1995a, 1995b, 1995c), Collier and Thomas (2007), Ovando, Combs and Collier (2006), and Thomas and Collier (1997). Overall, this model defines major developmental processes that children experience during their school years and that need to be supported at school for successful language acquisition and learning to take place. The model can be applied to native English speakers as well as to students acquiring English as their second language. Also, the Prism Model can be used to predict the major school factors that help to close the academic achievement gap in second language. Conceptually, here's how our research led to the Prism Model.

When we first began reporting on our research data and interpreting the results, we discussed second language proficiency development as the main reason for students' low performance. We emphasized the point that it takes many years to develop academic English. Now we have expanded our interpretation to include other factors. Second language acquisition is only one of many processes taking place in a complex, developmental process. But the main reason that it takes 4 to 10 years or more for English learners to reach grade-level performance on tests in English is that native English speakers are not standing still waiting for English learners to catch up with them (Thomas, 1992). Native English speakers are developing cognitively and academically with every year of school, as well as continuing their acquisition of their first language, English, in a learning environment that is favorable for instruction in English. School tests reflect ongoing linguistic, cognitive, and academic growth that occurs in an "English-friendly" learning environment.

The instructional situation for the native English speaker

Examining what happens developmentally to the native English speaker in school provides us with insights into the complex developmental processes also occurring for the non-native speaker of school age. It also helps us understand the results from the tests that we use to measure progress in school. All children experience natural, complex developmental processes that are ongoing throughout the school years. Two major developmental processes that occur at the subconscious level are linguistic and cognitive development, and these ongoing processes can be stimulated by consciously planned activities with teachers, parents, siblings, and friends.

Language and cognitive development go hand in hand. Language is the vehicle for communicating cognitively. In school, we develop students' cognitive growth through academic work across the curriculum in science, social studies, mathematics, language arts, and the fine arts. At home, parents naturally stimulate children's cognitive growth through daily, interactive problem-solving, family activities, and household responsibilities. All of this growth at home and school, conscious and subconscious, is reflected in the school tests, especially when long-term student progress is followed, with different tests of increasing difficulty for each age group or grade level. Teachers' tests change from week to week to reflect this expected growth. School district, state, and nationally normed tests also change from year to year to reflect this expected growth. Both the tests' content and presentation of items become more difficult with each succeeding school grade.

Native English speakers provide another perspective and additional insight on what the school tests measure and on how to understand the continuous process of first language development that is ongoing throughout the school years. Often it is assumed that the 5-year-old native English speaker entering school is fully proficient in the English language. This child is amazingly adept in using a complex oral language system, developed cognitively to the level of a 5-year-old. But even for the most gifted 5-year-old, much more than half of the English language remains to be acquired during the school years. Children from ages 6 to 12 continue to acquire (without being formally taught) subtleties in the phonological system, massive amounts of vocabulary, semantics (meaning), syntax (grammar), formal discourse patterns (stretches of language beyond a single sentence), and complex aspects of pragmatics (how language is used in a given context) in the oral system of the English language (Berko Gleason, 2009). Then there is the written system of English to be mastered across all of these same domains during the school years! Even an adolescent entering college must continue to acquire enormous amounts of vocabulary in every discipline of study and ongoing development of complex writing skills. (See Figure 4.1.)

Once again, the school tests reflect this expected English language growth with every year of schooling. In contrast, English learners taking an English-as-a-second-language proficiency test are being tested on a static measure. This is an important indicator of growth in each of the language domains for the first years of their English development, but their achievement is compared to a fixed standard of proficiency.

Thus when English learners take the school tests in English language arts and English reading, a very different type of test from the English proficiency test, they are being compared to and competing with a moving target, the native English speakers. In fact, the average score on the standardized, curricular tests is defined for each year and grade by the native English speaker who makes "1 year's progress in 1 year's time" and thus sets the standard for continuous progress for the English learner.

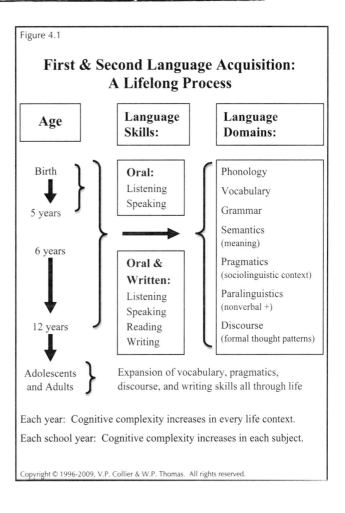

Figure 4.1

**First & Second Language Acquisition:
A Lifelong Process**

Age	**Language Skills:**	**Language Domains:**
Birth ↓ 5 years	**Oral:** Listening Speaking	Phonology Vocabulary Grammar Semantics (meaning)
6 years ↓ 12 years ↓	**Oral & Written:** Listening Speaking Reading Writing	Pragmatics (sociolinguistic context) Paralinguistics (nonverbal +) Discourse (formal thought patterns)
Adolescents and Adults ↓	Expansion of vocabulary, pragmatics, discourse, and writing skills all through life	

Each year: Cognitive complexity increases in every life context.

Each school year: Cognitive complexity increases in each subject.

The Prism Model: Language acquisition for school

The Prism Model has four major components that "drive" language acquisition for school: sociocultural, linguistic, academic, and cognitive processes. **A basic principle of the Prism Model is that linguistically diverse students who are not yet proficient in English need a school context that provides the same or equivalent basic conditions and advantages that the majority group experiences**. This includes attention to the ongoing developmental processes that occur naturally for any child all through the K–12 school years. For students who come from a bilingual community, these interdependent processes–nonstop cognitive, academic, and linguistic development–must occur in a supportive sociocultural environment through their first language and their second language to enhance student learning. Thus for bilingual learners, the Prism Model has four components for each language, comprising the sociocultural, linguistic, cognitive, and academic developmental processes for a total of eight dimensions. This is illustrated in Figure 4.2.

As you examine this figure, which looks triangular on the flat surface of the page, visualize instead that you are looking down through a complex multi-dimensional, sparkling prism, with the student in the center. Connected to the student's emotional responses to learning are the sociocultural processes that influence the learning process. Interconnected to this component are the other three major components–linguistic, academic, and cognitive processes–all four components interdependent and complex.

Sociocultural processes. At the heart of the Prism Model is the individual student going through the process of acquiring a second language in school. Central to that student's acquisition of language are all of the surrounding social and cultural processes occurring through everyday life within the student's past, present, and future, in all contexts—home, school, community, and the broader society. For example, sociocultural processes at work in second language acquisition may include individual students' emotional responses to school, such as self-esteem, anxiety, or other affective factors. At school, the instructional environment in a classroom or administrative program structure may create social and psychological distance between groups. Community or regional social patterns such as prejudice

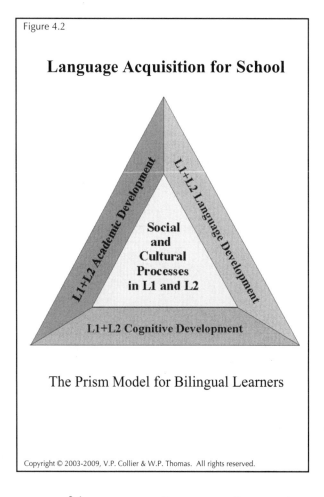

Figure 4.2

Language Acquisition for School

Social and Cultural Processes in L1 and L2

L1+L2 Academic Development

L1+L2 Language Development

L1+L2 Cognitive Development

The Prism Model for Bilingual Learners

and discrimination expressed towards groups or individuals in personal and professional contexts can influence students' achievement in school, as can societal patterns such as the subordinate status of a minority group, or acculturation versus assimilation forces at work. These factors can negatively influence the student's response to the new language and learning through the second language. Since the sociocultural environment at school is predominantly oriented toward the monolingual English-speaking student in a mostly English-speaking community, it is critical that we all continue to examine the differences in the sociocultural contexts for English learners and native English speakers as a cause of the observed achievement gap between these groups.

Language development. Linguistic processes, a second component of the model, consist of the subconscious aspects of language development (an innate ability all humans possess for acquisition of oral language), as well as the metalinguistic, conscious, formal teaching of language in school, and the acquisition of the written system of language. This includes the acquisition of the oral and written systems of the student's first language (L1) and second language (L2) across all language domains—phonology, vocabulary, morphology, syntax, semantics, pragmatics, discourse, and paralinguistics. To assure cognitive and academic success in the second language, a student's first language system, oral and written, must be developed to a high cognitive level at least throughout the elementary school years. We have compared the language development of English learners and native English speakers for differences that might lead to the observed achievement gap.

> At the 2003 La Cosecha conference, I heard Virginia Collier and Wayne Thomas present their findings on dual language learning. One of their findings stated that by the seventh, eighth, and ninth grades, children in dual language programs outperformed their monolingual peers. The information was invigorating because it gave even more validity to the importance of continuing to educate our children in our native language of Keres. ... With Cochiti Pueblo facing the very grave threat of losing our language, I thought that we must do more to support the community's desire to help children keep the language. ... With the support of the Cochiti Tribal Council, the board and I created the Keres Children's Learning Center (KCLC). The mission of KCLC is to create a linguistically and culturally rich learning environment that supports the fundamental principles and values of native life that are essential in socializing Cochiti Pueblo children ... KCLC is committed to providing a learning environment in which children hear Keres spoken naturally throughout the Center and in activities which reflect traditional practices in addition to preparing children for their future schooling.
>
> TRISHA MOQUINO
> COCHITI PUEBLO

Academic development. A third component of the model, academic development, includes all school work in language arts, mathematics, the sciences, social studies, and the fine arts, for each grade level, K–12 and beyond. With each succeeding grade, academic work dramatically expands the vocabulary, sociolinguistic, and discourse dimensions of language to higher cognitive levels. Academic knowledge and conceptual development transfer from the first language to the second language. Thus, it is most efficient to develop academic work through students' first language, while teaching the second language during other periods of the school day or week through meaningful academic content that reinforces and expands on the knowledge developed but does not repeat the academic work in first language. In earlier decades in the U.S., we emphasized teaching second language as the first step, and postponed the teaching of academics. However, research has shown that postponing or interrupting academic development while students work on acquiring the second language is likely to lead to academic failure in the long term. In an information-driven society that demands more knowledge processing with each succeeding year, English learners cannot afford the lost time, with native English speakers surging ahead in grade-level academic work, steadily making 1 year's progress in 1 year's time. Documenting the different experiences of English learners and native English speakers in academic development provides further explanation of the observed achievement gap.

Cognitive development. The fourth component of this model, the cognitive dimension, is a natural, subconscious process that occurs developmentally from birth to the end of schooling and beyond. An infant initially builds thought processes through interacting with loved ones in the language of the home. All parents (including those non-formally schooled) naturally stimulate children's L1 cognitive growth through daily interaction and family problem-solving in the language the parents know best. (See Figure 4.3.)

Figure 4.3

Cognitive Development at Home

An infant initially builds thought processes through interacting with loved ones in the language of the home (L1). This is important for building a cognitive knowledge base, and it is crucial to continue that L1 cognitive development through age 11-12. At home, parents naturally stimulate children's L1 cognitive growth through:

Daily interactive problem-solving:

- asking questions
- making decisions
- discussing daily activities
- moral support
- setting goals
- sharing values

Household responsibilities:

- shopping
- cooking
- family budgets
- cleaning, laundry

Family activities:

- telling stories, sharing family heritage
- sharing music, art, games, sports
- reading books together
- going places together
- celebrating together

Students bring 5 to 6 years of cognitive development in their L1 to their first day of school. This is a knowledge base, an important stepping stone to build on as cognitive development continues. It is extremely important that cognitive development continue through a child's first language at least through the elementary school years. Extensive research has demonstrated that children who reach full cognitive development in two languages (generally reaching the threshold in L1 by around age 11–12) enjoy cognitive advantages over monolinguals, resulting in higher academic success. (See Figure 4.4.)

Cognitive development was mostly neglected by second language educators in the U.S. until the past decade. Language teaching curricula were simplified, structured, and sequenced during the 1970s, and when academic content was added to language lessons in the 1980s, academics were watered down into cognitively simple tasks, often under the label of "basic skills." Too often neglected was the crucial role of cognitive development in the first language. Now we know from the growing research base that educators must address linguistic, cognitive, and academic development equally, through both first and second languages, if they are to assure students' academic success in the second language. This is especially necessary if English learners are ever to reach full parity in all curricular areas with native English speakers.

Interdependence of the four components. All of these four components—sociocultural, academic, cognitive, and linguistic—are interdependent. If one is developed to the neglect of another, this may be detrimental to a student's overall growth and future success. Also, the academic, cognitive, and linguistic components must be viewed as natural developmental processes. For the child, adolescent, and young adult still attending formal schooling, development of any one of the three academic, cognitive, and linguistic components depends critically on the simultaneous

Figure 4.4

Research Generalizations: The Relationship Between First Language Development and Cognitive Development

When a child's first language (L1) development is discontinued before it is completed, the child may experience negative cognitive effects in second language (L2) development. Conversely, a child who has reached full cognitive development in two languages enjoys cognitive advantages over monolingual peers.

Consistent, uninterrupted cognitive and academic development in all subjects throughout a student's schooling is more important than the number of instructional hours in the child's second language for ensuring successful academic achievement in a second language.

The more L1 instruction provided across the curriculum combined with balanced L2 instruction across the curriculum, the higher students achieve academically in L2 when compared to matched student groups schooled monolingually in L2.

development of the other two, through both first and second languages. At the same time, sociocultural processes strongly influence students' access to these three components, in both positive and negative ways. It is crucial that educators provide a socioculturally supportive school environment, allowing natural language, academic, and cognitive development to flourish in both first and second languages.

First language and cognitive development. To give an important example of the interwoven nature of all the components of the Prism Model, let's examine the relationship between a child's first language and cognitive development. First language development is deeply interrelated with cognitive development, as thousands of studies in educational psychology and linguistics have shown. Children who stop cognitive development in the first language before they have reached the final Piagetian stage of formal operations (somewhere around puberty) typically experience lower academic achievement. Many studies indicate that if students do not reach a certain threshold in their first language, they may experience cognitive difficulties in the second language (Baker, 2006; Bialystok, 1991, 2001; Collier, 1987; Collier & Thomas, 1989; Cummins, 1976, 1981, 1991, 2000; Dulay & Burt, 1980; Duncan & De Avila, 1979; González, 2005; Skutnabb-Kangas, 1981; Thomas & Collier, 1997, 2002).

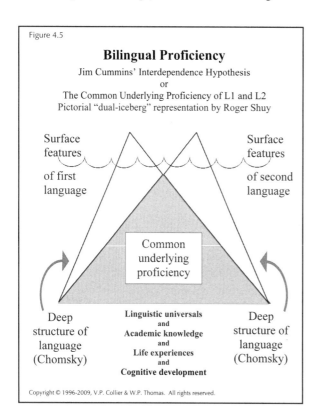

Figure 4.5

Bilingual Proficiency

Jim Cummins' Interdependence Hypothesis
or
The Common Underlying Proficiency of L1 and L2
Pictorial "dual-iceberg" representation by Roger Shuy

Surface features of first language

Surface features of second language

Common underlying proficiency

Deep structure of language (Chomsky)

Linguistic universals
and
Academic knowledge
and
Life experiences
and
Cognitive development

Deep structure of language (Chomsky)

Furthermore, developing cognitively and linguistically in first language at least throughout the elementary school years provides a knowledge base that transfers from first language to second language. Figure 4.5 illustrates the interdependence between a student's first and second languages and the deep knowledge that automatically transfers from one language to the other.

The image symbolizes a student's two languages as two overlapping icebergs, where above the ocean surface the icebergs appear to be separate and distinct. But the large majority of an iceberg is under water. When you study the surface structure of a language, you find that there is a deeper, underlying structure, and at the deep level there is more in common across all languages of the world than that which is different. So when students develop their first language to full adult proficiency, it is a resource or knowledge base for all other languages the student acquires.

When schooling is provided in both first and second languages, both languages are the vehicle for strong cognitive and academic development. Linguistically, deep structure in the first language transfers to the second language. More than half of all literacy skills transfer from first language to second language, even when the first language is a non-Roman-alphabet language and the second language is English. Schools do not need to re-teach reading in the second language when students are already literate in their first language (Chu, 1981; Cummins, 1991, 2000; Freeman & Freeman, 2006; Goldenberg, 2008; Pérez, 2004; Thonis, 1994). Also, academic knowledge transfers from first language to second language. If a student has taken a calculus course in Korean, he does not need to repeat that course in English–the skills transfer and can be demonstrated on a test, once the student has acquired the English vocabulary to express what he already knows.

Moreover, cognitive processes developed in the first language transfer to the second language (Baker, 2006, 2007; Bialystok, 1991, 2001; González, 2005 Grosjean, 1982; Tokuhama-Espinosa, 2003). Life experiences in a child's first language are a knowledge base, a resource that stimulates cognition. Even when children experience something as devastating as war, the problem-solving skills that emerge from day-to-day survival are a resource for future adult life. Yet it clearly is not necessary to re-experience war in the second language for them to have access to the thinking skills developed in the first language.

Additive vs. subtractive bilingualism. Another example of the interdependence of the components of the Prism Model comes from the concept of additive and subtractive bilingualism introduced by the field of sociolinguistics (Lambert, 1975, 1984). Around the world, the school achievement of children who belong to ethnolinguistic minorities can be heavily influenced by the societal relationships that exist between majority and minority groups. These societal relationships are linked to attitudes toward the minority languages spoken by these linguistic communities. (See Figure 4.6.)

In bilingual contexts where additive bilingualism is taking place, students do just fine in school. So, for example, a native English speaker in the U.S. attending classes in Spanish is automatically in an additive bilingual context. She is adding Spanish to her linguistic repertoire at no cost to her English, which is supported and nurtured by the broader society. If she develops both languages to a high academic level, in 4 to 7 years, she will be able to outscore monolinguals on school tests. Additive bilingualism leads to many cognitive advantages, including greater

Additive vs. Subtractive Bilingualism

Additive Bilingualism: L1 *plus* L2

As you acquire your second language, you continue to develop cognitively in your first language. You develop age-appropriate proficiency in both L1 and L2.

The result: Positive cognitive effects.
Proficient bilinguals outscore monolinguals on school tests.

Subtractive Bilingualism: L2 *minus* L1

As you acquire your second language, you gradually lose your first language.

The result: Negative cognitive effects.
Subtractive bilinguals do less well in school as cognitive complexity increases in the school curriculum.

(Concept from Wallace Lambert, sociolinguist)

flexibility in thinking and more varied problem-solving skills.

In contrast, subtractive bilingualism leads to cognitive loss (Skutnabb-Kangas & Cummins, 1988; Wong Fillmore, 1991b). When students are gradually losing their first language while acquiring the second language, they may suffer negative cognitive consequences, especially if their first language is stopped before cognitive development is completed by age 11 or 12. Groups of students in subtractive bilingual situations, such as immigrants being forced to lose their first language at a very young age, do less well in school. The U.S. is a very subtractive bilingual society (Tse, 2001). Yet schools can reverse this pattern, leading to full achievement gap closure in English for all students, by providing academic and cognitive support for students in an additive bilingual school context.

The instructional situation for the English learner in an English-only program

Using all the components of the Prism Model, we can apply this research knowledge base to the varying school programs provided for English learners in the United States. This comparison will make clear where the school experience of English learners differs from that of native English speakers and becomes a contributing factor to the achievement gap. Figure 4.7 portrays the common view of many U.S. education policy makers—that students must learn English first.

From a common-sense perspective, it would seem obvious that the first step anyone should take when entering a new country is to learn the language of that country. This is indeed a wise decision for a cognitively mature adult who has already mastered the requisite academic material to an adult level in first language. The adult immigrant who has been formally schooled has completed development in two of the Prism components–cognitive and academic development–and lacks only one dimension of the linguistic component, acquisition of the second language, having already acquired first language to adult level of proficiency.

But the school-age child is in a very different situation. Developmental processes must continue nonstop all through the school years in order for a child to reach the cognitive maturity of an adult. Academic development must continue nonstop through the school years for full adult mastery of the academic curriculum to occur. While learning English is critically important, English is only one part of the learning process. When learning English is emphasized and mastery of the curriculum is ignored or de-emphasized, the full Prism Model of language acquisition for school is reduced to a partial focus on one dimension, development of the second language, English. The other half of that component is missing—the continuing development of first language. Thus, an emphasis on learning English above all else has detrimental consequences for the student in three out of four of the Prism Model's components.

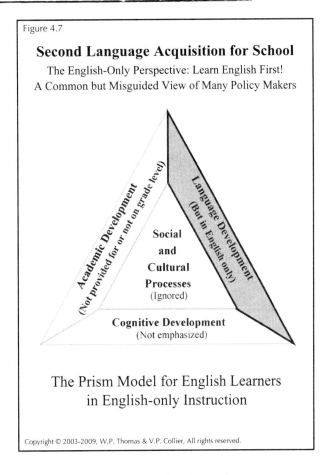

Figure 4.7

Second Language Acquisition for School

The English-Only Perspective: Learn English First!
A Common but Misguided View of Many Policy Makers

The Prism Model for English Learners
in English-only Instruction

First, meaningful academic development is not provided for in the initial years, because the highest priority is learning English rather than academic content. In succeeding years, academic development is often not on grade level, because students studying only in their second language have missed at least 2 years of academic work while acquiring a basic knowledge of the new language.

Second, cognitive development is not emphasized in the second language and is not provided for in the first language at school. Students are not classic "tabula rasa" (blank slates) on their first day of school. Rather, they enter school with 6 years of life experiences which significantly impact cognitive development in their first language. These students must continue to develop cognitively at the same rate as do native-English-speaking students in their native language. However, switching a student's language of instruction to all-English causes a cognitive slowdown for English learners that can last for several years. During this period, the native English speakers continue to develop cognitively at normal rates, but the English learners fall behind in cognitive development and may never catch up to the constantly advancing native English speakers.

Third, in an English-only environment, sociocultural processes may be largely ignored, or less well provided for. Thus when English learners feel that they are not in a supportive environment, less learning takes place. In summary, an emphasis on learning English above all else subjects English learners to reduced academic and cognitive development, low self-esteem, and less motivation for learning in an unfavorable school environment. This leads to less mastery of the curriculum and, ironically, less mastery of English!

The Prism Model for the native-English-speaking student

Now contrast this with the situation of the native English speaker. For most native English speakers, all four dimensions of the Prism Model are in place in the students' first language, including schooling in a socioculturally supportive environment, and nonstop cognitive and linguistic development in the first language. (See Figure 4.8.)

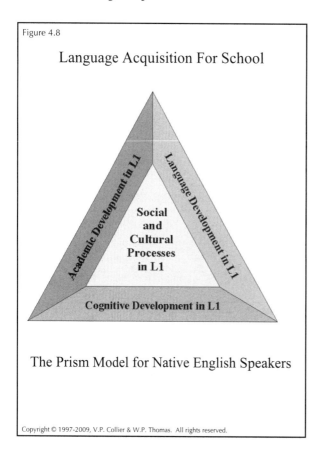

Figure 4.8

Language Acquisition For School

Academic Development in L1

Language Development in L1

Social and Cultural Processes in L1

Cognitive Development in L1

The Prism Model for Native English Speakers

From kindergarten on, native English speakers are instructed in all school subjects through English, the language in which they are cognitively mature for their age. Even for those who choose to participate in a bilingual class, they do not fall behind in other school subjects while learning another language during the school years.

Typical native speakers of English make 10 months' progress in school achievement for each 10-month school year. This performance defines the 50th percentile or normal curve equivalent (NCE–an equal-interval percentile) on standardized norm-referenced tests and the average score on grade-level criterion-referenced tests as the students progress from grade to grade. These tests measure continuous linguistic, cognitive, and academic growth in English, and the tests change weekly, monthly, and yearly to reflect that growth.

How academic progress is measured for both native and non-native speakers of English

It is on these school tests administered in English that we unrealistically expect English learners to be able to demonstrate miraculous growth. Policy makers assume that non-English-proficient students should somehow be able to leap from the first percentile or NCE to the 50th (as compared to native speakers of English) in 1 to 2 years. During this period, the native speakers continue to make 10 months' progress in 10 months' time. Yet if English learners are being taught only in English, a language they do not yet understand, they need at least 2 to 3 years to reach a high enough level of proficiency in their second language to attempt to keep pace with the native English speaker in school. And during these 2 to 3 years of development in English, they lose instructional ground to the advantaged native English speaker. This achievement gap may never be closed.

For example, one group of non-English-proficient students might study English intensively, and by the end of their first 2 years, they make an enormous leap from the first to the 20th NCE when they first take a standardized test in English reading, English language arts, and mathematics. To score at the level of the typical native English speaker (50th percentile or NCE) in all school subjects, these English learners must then continue to make more than 1 year's progress in 1 year's time and do so for several consecutive years to ever close the initial gap of 25–30 NCEs from the 20th to the 50th NCE. Figures 3.1 and 3.2 in the previous chapter visually illustrate this point. For English learners, progress at the typical rate of native English speakers means only maintaining the initial large gap, not closing it, as the native English speakers continue to make additional progress in all Prism components with each passing year. If English learners make less than typical native English speaker progress (e.g., English learners might make 6 months' progress in one 10-month school year while typical native speakers make 10 months' progress), the initial large achievement gap will widen even further.

To illustrate further, if a group of English learners experiences an initial 3 year gap in achievement assessed in English (math, science, social studies, language arts, reading, writing), they must make an average of about 1½ years' progress in the next 6 consecutive years (for a total of 9 years' progress in 6 years–a 30-NCE gain, from the 20th to the 50th NCE) to reach the same long-term performance level that a typical native English speaker reaches by making 1 year's progress in 1 year's time for each of 6 years (for a total of 6 years' progress in 6 years—a 0-NCE gain, staying at the 50th NCE). This is a difficult task indeed, even for an English learner who has received excellent formal schooling before entering U.S. schools and whose achievement is on grade level for his/her age when tested in his/her native language. Still more daunting is the task of the English learner whose schooling has been interrupted by social or economic upheaval or warfare, a typical case among recent immigrants. Learning English while keeping up with native speakers' progress in other school subjects and while making up the material lost to interrupted or non-existent schooling in the student's native country is a truly formidable undertaking. Such students require many years of very effective school programs to fully close the achievement gap.

It is for these reasons that on-grade-level bilingual schooling is essential to these students' long-term academic success. While the bilingual student is making the gains needed with each succeeding year to close the gap in performance on the tests in English, that student is not getting behind in cognitive and academic development, unlike his counterpart in English-only instruction. Once the bilingual students' average achievement reaches the 50th percentile or NCE on the school tests in English, the cognitive and academic work in first language has kept these students on grade level and they sustain grade-level performance in English even as the academic work gets increasingly complex with each succeeding year in middle and high school, just as on-grade-level native English speakers do.

Furthermore, first language development at school is deeply interrelated with cognitive development. As noted earlier, children who stop cognitive development in first language before they have reached age 11 or 12 run the risk of suffering negative consequences, as measured by school tests. Developing cognitively and linguistically in first language at home and at school at least throughout the elementary school years provides a knowledge base that transfers from first to second language. When schooling is provided through two languages, both languages become the vehicle for strong cognitive and academic development, accelerating students' academic achievement and eventually closing the achievement gap.

Thus, the simplistic notion—that all we need to do is to teach English learners the English language—does not address the full needs of the school-age child. Furthermore, when we teach only the English language, we are literally slowing down a child's cognitive and academic growth, as well as ignoring the sociocultural aspects of learning. This creates a performance gap for the English learner, and that child may never catch up to the constantly advancing native English speaker!

Analyzing your school and school district

It can be helpful to consider planning or role-playing your response to questions and concerns from within the school, district, or larger community. This allows you to be prepared and confident when challenges occur.

Scenario A: School board meeting

John: *So I just don't get it! When I worked for the U.S. government, to get the next overseas assignment to Poland, I got sent to language school and within 2 years I mastered a pretty sophisticated knowledge of Polish. Why can't these kids do that?!*

Emma: *Okay, think about it, John, from the Prism Model perspective. Had you finished school?*

John: *Well, I had a master's degree.*

Emma: *So you were cognitively and academically mature. And you had nonstop cognitive development in your first language. Furthermore, when you went to the language school to learn Polish, you were being paid by the government to do that—socioculturally you were fully supported. In fact, you were probably given a raise for your studies in Polish. So you had all the bases covered. All you needed was the second language.*

Scenario B: Staff lounge (at an elementary school)

Fifth grade teacher: *Our middle school provides instruction only in English. I just don't feel right continuing to teach in both languages. I really need to get these kids ready for next year.*

Colleague: *I know it's tempting to spend more time developing their English at this point, but research supporting this Prism Model shows that language and content development in the students' first language is really key to their success ... and the more the better. Are we undermining the kindergarten through fourth grade dual language experience if we let it go now? We're seeing progress ...*

Fifth grade teacher: *I just worry about the kids, and I want to do well by them. The pressure is on all of us for them to achieve on the English assessments, and after this year, English is all they will get.*

Colleague: *That might be the best reason not to eliminate home language instruction in fifth grade. What if we use our grade level meetings to really focus on how we can better support transfer of language and literacy skills across the two languages? Maybe by planning together, we can also do a better job of creating some redundancy in content learning, without just repeating the same thing ...*

Reflections from the Field

After 12 years of implementation, Connecting Worlds/Mundos Unidos, a Two-Way Dual Language Immersion Gifted/Talented (GT) Magnet Program (Grades K–12), has succeeded in providing all students it serves a high quality education, especially those who have been under-identified and under-served (ELLs and Economically Disadvantaged) in the world of GT. During the development of the program, one of the most powerful and comprehensive studies which helped us recognize the benefits of dual language was that of Dr. Virginia Collier and Dr. Wayne Thomas. Due to their research and dissemination of findings, we felt confident in providing our students an accelerated and rigorous academic dual language program, through which they would become proficient, bilingual, and biliterate in English and Spanish.

Laila Rizk Ferris, Principal, and Sandra P. Spivey, Assistant Principal
Mesita Elementary School, El Paso Independent School District
El Paso, Texas

CHAPTER FIVE: PROGRAM EFFECTIVENESS

Now that we understand why it takes many years for any group of students who initially score at very low levels to reach grade-level achievement, the next step is to identify program characteristics that accelerate English learners' growth and thereby close the gap with time. We shall then illustrate how each of the major programs for English learners implements these effective program characteristics in different ways and at different levels. We will use the dimensions of the Prism Model as an organizer for this review of program characteristics. Finally, we will review the program effectiveness research in bilingual/multicultural/ESL education, to understand the short-term and long-term results of each program type, as measured by student achievement on all subject tests in English through the end of high school.

Characteristics of effective programs

In the following sections, we discuss six major characteristics of effective programs for English learners. These are drawn from the results of our longitudinal research, the Prism Model, and other researchers' work. In the latter part of the chapter, we will analyze each major program model developed for English learners in the U.S. with respect to these characteristics of effective programs. The six are: (1) long term, (2) instruction through the first language, (3) instruction through the second language, (4) sociocultural support, (5) interactive, cognitively challenging, discovery learning, and (6) integration with the mainstream.

Long term. We have found in our national research that gap closure for English learners occurs only while they are attending special bilingual/ESL support programs. Thus it is crucial to create effective, academically challenging programs that accelerate students' growth, assisting them to make more than 1 year's progress every year for several years in a row. The short term (1 to 3 years of support) does not close the gap. The long term (6 or more years) is an essential characteristic of effective programs that fully close the gap. In addition, because of the long time needed, programs must be designed as an integral part of the instructional mainstream, not as isolated classrooms where ESL students are separated from their peers for many years. (See Figure 5.1 for an overview of comparisons of gains in typical, effective, and outstanding programs for linguistically diverse students.)

Instruction through the first language. It is very clear from all our research findings on long-term program effectiveness, and consistently confirmed in other researchers' studies, that when English learners have the opportunity to do academic work through the medium of their first language, in the long term they are academically more successful in their second language. In all of our studies

Program Effectiveness and Gap Closure

Typical size of initial achievement gap between
English learners and native English speakers:
25-30 NCEs*

Expected NCE gains each year for:

- Typical native-English speakers   0   NCEs
  (making "one year's progress in one year")
- Students in a **typical** program for English learners   1-3   NCEs
- Students in an **effective** program for English learners 4-6   NCEs
- Students in an **outstanding** program for English learners 7-9 NCEs
  (This 7-9 NCE gain is very rare.)

Number of years needed to close the gap:

- a typical program   8-12 years
- an effective program   5-6 years
- an outstanding program   3-4 years

Question: Does your instructional program for English
learners close the achievement gap in 5-6 years and keep it
closed in later years?

*Normal Curve Equivalents (NCEs) are equal-sized national percentiles.

in 35 school districts in 16 states, we have found the following patterns which strongly support academic development of the primary language for as many years as possible. First, students who emigrated to the U.S. around age 11, after having received at least 4 years of on-grade-level primary language schooling in their home country, made greater progress than similar groups of students who emigrated during preschool years and received all their schooling in English in the U.S. Second, students born in the U.S. who received 2 to 3 years of bilingual schooling made greater progress than similar students who received all of their schooling in English including ESL support for 2 to 3 years. Third, students who were born in the U.S. and received 5 to 6 years of on-grade-level bilingual schooling in U.S. schools made greater progress than similar groups who received only 2 to 3 years of bilingual schooling in U.S. schools.

Comparing all of these groups receiving support services that differed chiefly by the amount of first language academic support, the message from our findings is overwhelmingly clear that all linguistically diverse groups benefit enormously in the long-term from on-grade-level academic work in their first language, for as many years as possible. The more children develop their first language academically and cognitively at an age-appropriate level, the more successful they will be in academic achievement in English by the end of their school years. If learning English is an important instructional goal (and of course it is), full proficiency in academic English (as opposed to only social English or partial English language proficiency) is enhanced by long-term bilingual programs.

It is important here to remember that these findings are different from short-term findings, which offer misleading results. Many studies of school effectiveness in bilingual/ESL education have focused on a short-term look at Grades K–3. And many of these studies have concluded that there is little difference between programs in the early grades. We found similar patterns in our data, but as we continued to follow groups of students through the middle and high school years, we found very large, cumulative, long-term differences in student achievement that were directly attributable to the type of program services that they received during their elementary school years (e.g., see Figure 5.2 presented later in this chapter). We have concluded that first language cognitive and academic development is a key predictor of long-term academic success in the second language, English.

It is also important to remember that this predictor is much more powerful when first language is developed through academically challenging, age-appropriate schooling in first language. Some forms of bilingual education in the U.S. have focused on minimal first language support, such as only providing first language literacy development. While any first language development is beneficial, for students to get the full power of this predictor they need to be challenged academically across the curriculum through their first language. They need to do cognitively complex school tasks appropriate for their age in their first language.

While the schools should provide support for first language cognitive development, it is possible that parents can also provide some of this first language cognitive and academic support at home. We have some survey data that suggests that parents who have completed at least a high school degree do try to provide some extra first language support. But parents who work long hours to be income providers find this parental role increasingly difficult. When schools can provide first language cognitive and academic support, all linguistically diverse students will greatly benefit. This predictor holds true for immigrants to the U.S., as well as for U.S.-born linguistically diverse students. First language schooling is powerful for students who have lost their home language, for bilingual students who are very proficient in both their home language and English, and for students who are just beginning development of English.

Instruction through the second language—English. The type of second language instructional support is the key to this third predictor having some power. During the portion of the school day that is taught through English as a second language, we have found that it is not enough just to teach the English language. More English grammar instruction is not productive, because a second language is best learned by using the language in a meaningful context. When English as a second language is used to provide students access to the full curriculum, science experiments and math problem-solving bring meaning to the English lessons. But

ESL taught through academic content must also be provided in a socioculturally supportive environment, while challenging students to work at age-appropriate level through their second language.

Just as with first language instructional support, the second language component of the day should be taught through cognitively complex academic work across the curriculum, while making the material meaningful for students at their proficiency level in English. Thus in our research findings, students who received ESL taught through academic content (by teachers trained in second language acquisition and the content area who were also socioculturally supportive of students) made greater progress than students receiving ESL classes focused on the teaching of the English language and the remaining English portion of the day in mainstream classes. Students who received first and second language academic content (again, taught by teachers trained in second language acquisition and the content areas who were also socioculturally supportive of students) did better than students who received only second language academic work. We will discuss time spent in the English mainstream in the sixth section on program characteristics.

Sociocultural support. Sociocultural support is a difficult predictor to measure, but in general we have attempted to analyze its influence through interviews with school staff that help us identify classes and schools where students feel strongly supported as contrasted with places where students feel insecure. We have found that student academic achievement is highest when the bilingual/ESL staff at a given school feel very positive about the school environment, including the general level of administrative and teaching staff support and the context for intercultural knowledge-building provided for linguistically diverse students. This finding is reflected in other researchers' work (e.g. Cummins, 2000; Gold, 2006; Henze, Katz, Norte, Sather & Walker, 2002; Jaramillo & Olsen, 1999; Lucas, Henze & Donato, 1990; McLeod, 1996; Moll, Vélez-Ibáñez, Greenberg & Rivera, 1990; Tharp & Gallimore, 1988).

In our research studies, we found that bilingual/ESL staff identified certain schools as highly socioculturally supportive. Linguistically diverse students in these schools are respected and valued for the rich life experiences in other cultural contexts that they bring to the classroom. Their bicultural experience is considered a knowledge base for teachers to build on. For them, the school is a safe, secure environment for learning. Native English speakers treat linguistically diverse students with respect, and there is less discrimination, prejudice, and open hostility. Often, sociocultural support includes an additive, enrichment bilingual context for schooling, where students' first language is affirmed, respected, valued, used for cognitive and academic development, and used to help students acquire full academic English, not just "playground English." Sometimes native English speakers choose to join the bilingual classes, and both groups work together at all times in an integrated schooling context. In general, we have found that the school buildings with the strongest sociocultural support for linguistically diverse students are those that produce student graduates who are among the highest academic achievers in each school district.

Interactive, cognitively challenging, discovery learning. We and other researchers have found that across all program types, students who participate in classes that are very interactive, with hands-on problem-solving facilitated by teachers so that students work cooperatively together in a socioculturally supportive environment, do better academically than those attending classes taught more traditionally. Teachers in the focus groups in our studies expressed excitement when staff development sessions assisted them with cooperative learning, thematic lessons, literacy development across the curriculum, process writing, performance and portfolio assessment, uses of technology, multiple intelligences, critical thinking, learning strategies, and global perspectives infused into the curriculum.

Sometimes remedial classes can become quite isolated from the curricular mainstream, leading to lowered cognitive complexity of lessons and lower expectations for students' progress. When this happens, the emergence of an achievement gap is virtually guaranteed. But when bilingual/ESL classes are viewed from an enrichment perspective as cognitively challenging, accelerated learning, then students and teachers can work together to tackle complex issues and problem-solving tasks across the curriculum and the achievement gap begins to close. So the predictor here is for students to be challenged with cognitively complex work that is age-appropriate, with access to all subject matter—integrated language arts, literature, math, science, social studies, and the fine arts—through meaningful lessons that provide for interactive, discovery learning, with students teaching each other and the teacher facilitating the process.

Integration with the mainstream. Cost-effectiveness and the duplication of existing services are issues that greatly concern every school administrator. Do all linguistically diverse students need add-on services, or can effective support be provided in grade-level classes? We have found that bilingual/ESL program models that find ways to integrate with grade-level classes in the mainstream instructional program can be highly effective, if they are carefully planned and implemented by well-trained bilingual/ESL school staff. But this does not mean submersion in the mainstream classroom. Second language students participating in a mainstream program need substantial support from well-trained teachers who understand the second language acquisition process and who support, respect, and value bilingual/bicultural learners.

The curricular mainstream for native English speakers serves several important functions for bilingual/ESL staff. For natural second language acquisition to occur, English learners need access to meaningful interaction with native-English-speaking peers in a supportive environment with teachers who are trained to facilitate the learning of both groups. Same-age peers are a crucial source of second language input. But English-speaking peers are only beneficial in a social setting that brings students together cooperatively (Wong Fillmore, 1991a), including interactive negotiation of meaning and equally shared academic tasks. The teacher serves an important role in structuring the class tasks so that the second language acquisition process is enhanced, and teachers need to be well trained to provide the sociocultural support for all students. How can schools accomplish this when bilingual teachers are in short supply? Teaming of bilingual/ESL staff with grade-level teachers is one strategy used in some of the schools in our research sites. However, administrators must include extensive planning time in the school schedule when team teaching is the instructional and professional expectation. Ongoing staff development for all teachers on meeting English learners' needs is another important strategy.

A second function of the curricular mainstream is to continue the cognitive challenge. Student groups who are separated from grade-level classes for most of the school day for several years do not know the level of cognitive and academic work expected in the mainstream, and with time, students may develop lower aspirations for their own academic achievement. Also, teachers who want English learners to be successful may inadvertently "water down" instruction to make it easier for the students. Many researchers have documented how ability grouping, tracking, and other forms of segregation can lead to students' social perceptions of inadequacy and eventually to low achievement (e.g. Callahan, 2005; Hargreaves, 1997; Jacob & Jordan, 1993; Oakes, 1985, 1990, 1992; Oakes, Quartz, Ryan & Lipton, 2000). The schools in our research sites with higher academic achievement have eliminated most forms of ability grouping and tracking. They have found meaningful ways to school students together, for at least half of each school day, and in some programs, for the whole day. In these programs, both native English speakers and English learners score higher than their counterparts not attending such programs.

In our research findings, the program with the highest long-term academic success is two-way dual language education. This is an integrated form of bilingual education in which native English speakers and English learners may participate. Since this is a mainstream, grade-level model of schooling, it is the most cost-effective model of bilingual education, because add-on services do not need to be provided by extra staff. We will examine this model in the next section, where we illustrate the five program characteristics just discussed as they apply to some common program models in bilingual/ESL education.

English learners' long-term academic achievement

To examine the long-term perspective from kindergarten through twelfth grade, in our research studies conducted from 1985 to the present, we have examined large cohorts of English learners of similar student background, following them for as long as they remained in each school system. The figures in this chapter from our research findings illustrate English learners' achievement across many school districts from all regions of the U.S. These are students who start U.S. schooling with no proficiency in English, but by the end of their schooling they are classified as English-proficient. In our analyses, we have followed their progress after they leave the special program designed to help them learn English and they have moved into the English mainstream. After English learners have moved into the mainstream, we classify them as *former English learners* or simply *linguistically diverse students*.

Most of our figures focus on former English learners' long-term performance on norm-referenced tests in English reading. Norm-referenced tests are generally the most difficult of all tests, as they correlate strongly at the eleventh grade level with the reading test of the SAT, a college entrance exam. The reading test measures problem-solving and thinking skills across the curriculum. We have chosen this type of test as a measure of our long-term goal, since these students will be denied access to continuing studies at university level if they do not reach at least a minimal level of achievement on this test by the end of high school. Our ultimate goal is equal educational opportunity for all, including access to higher education.

In addition, we are analyzing patterns in all regions of the United States, and norm-referenced tests allow educators to compare student achievement across all the states. Some students from your state will attend universities in other regions of the country, and this more difficult test shows the true size of the gap, in comparison to students throughout the U.S. The state curricular tests vary greatly in level of difficulty and cannot be used for comparison purposes beyond each state. (See Appendix A for more on state tests.)

In our findings, patterns of student performance on the norm-referenced tests in science and social studies fall into the same general pattern as the English reading test. Mathematics and English language arts achievement scores of former English learners are slightly higher than their performance on the English reading, science, and social studies tests, but the same general pattern of performance, as well as the same ranking of long-term achievement influenced by program participation, is present in the mathematics and language arts data.

In general, when examining the two curricular areas on the standardized tests that focus on the English language—reading and language arts—we have found that the language arts tests tend to measure more easy-to-teach discrete-point skills; whereas the reading tests involve more complex problem-solving across the curriculum. The reading test is thus the most demanding—the "ultimate measure"— of all the curricular subtests of the standardized tests. When English learners are able to reach age-appropriate grade-level norms on the reading subtest and sustain that level of achievement in subsequent years, they have demonstrated that they can compete successfully with native English speakers on the most difficult test given in school. More importantly, this is an indicator that they are moving toward true long-term educational parity with native English speakers in all subjects, the ultimate goal for educating English learners.

Strongest predictor: Type of program provided in elementary school

Figure 5.2 provides an overview of all of our research findings from 1985 to the present, comparing seven program types provided during the elementary school years. When we first published this figure in 1997, it was based on over 42,317 longitudinal student records. We have now conducted many additional studies, which have continued to confirm the general patterns and program rankings found in this figure, after having analyzed over 6.2 million student records, in urban, suburban, and rural school districts in all regions of the U.S., demonstrating that our findings presented in this figure are applicable almost everywhere. In research terms, our findings are very generalizable in all regions and contexts of the United States.

Figure 5.2 presents the academic achievement of English learners who begin schooling in the U.S. in kindergarten with no proficiency in English. These students do not remain English learners throughout their schooling, but they are all ESL beginners when they enter U.S. schools in kindergarten. This figure presents cohorts of students who start kindergarten with the same general background characteristics—i.e., no proficiency in English and low socioeconomic status as measured by eligibility for free or reduced lunch.

Each solid line in Figure 5.2 represents English learners who received one type of special program designed to assist them with learning English, beginning in kindergarten. These special programs differed in their degree of use of effective strategies for educating English learners. The special program lasted from 2 to 7 years, depending upon what type of program it was. These students then continued in the mainstream in grade-level classes with instruction all in English through the remainder of their elementary school years and throughout their middle and high school years.

Number of years of instruction is considered a part of the program's definition, and not a variable to be controlled or manipulated. This is because the instructional

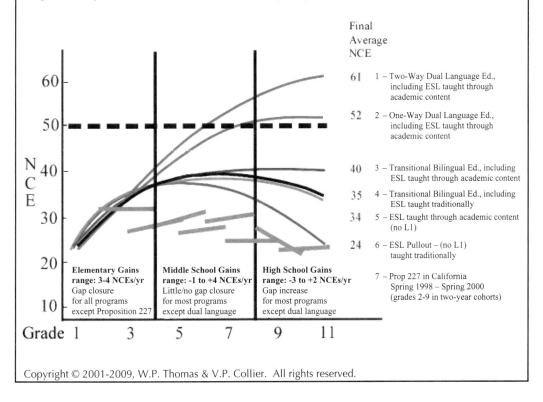

Figure 5.2

English Learners' Long-Term K–12 Achievement
in Normal Curve Equivalents (NCEs)
on Standardized Tests in English Reading
Compared across Seven Program Models

Results aggregated from longitudinal studies of well-implemented,
mature programs in five school districts and in California.

Program 1: Two-way Dual Language Education (DLE), including ESL taught through academic content

Program 2: One-way DLE, including ESL taught through academic content

Program 3: Transitional Bilingual Ed., including ESL taught through academic content

Program 4: Transitional Bilingual Ed., including ESL, taught traditionally

Program 5: ESL taught through academic content using current approaches with no L1 use

Program 6: ESL pullout - taught by pullout from mainstream classroom with no L1 use

Program 7: Proposition 227 in California (successive 2-year quasi-longitudinal cohorts)

Final
Average
NCE

61   1 – Two-Way Dual Language Ed.,
          including ESL taught through
          academic content

52   2 – One-Way Dual Language Ed.,
          including ESL taught through
          academic content

40   3 – Transitional Bilingual Ed., including
          ESL taught through academic content

35   4 – Transitional Bilingual Ed., including
          ESL taught traditionally

34   5 – ESL taught through academic content
          (no L1)

24   6 – ESL Pullout – (no L1)
          taught traditionally

      7 – Prop 227 in California
          Spring 1998 – Spring 2000
          (grades 2-9 in two-year cohorts)

Elementary Gains
range: 3-4 NCEs/yr
Gap closure
for all programs
except Proposition 227

Middle School Gains
range: -1 to +4 NCEs/yr
Little/no gap closure
for most programs
except dual language

High School Gains
range: -3 to +2 NCEs/yr
Gap increase
for most programs
except dual language

intent is quite different from one program type to another. For example, ESL pull-out programs (Line 6) are designed to be short term, 1 to 2 years of instructional support from an ESL-certified teacher for 1 to 2 hours of each day. Thus, there are no 4-year, 5-year, or 6-year ESL-pullout programs in existence in our research sites. ESL pullout is, by definition, a program that is short term and of low instructional intensity. Since ESL-pullout programs address only one Prism Model dimension, learning the English language, and do not explicitly provide for students' continuing age-appropriate development in cognitive and academic areas while they are learning English, it is instructionally desirable that students have shorter exposure to such programs.

In contrast, dual language programs (Lines 1 and 2) are designed to allow the students to continue age-appropriate development in all school subjects and to maintain native-speaker-like rates of cognitive development through first language instruction while they are acquiring academic English. Thus, there are no 1-year, 2-year, 3-year, or 4-year dual language programs in our participating school systems. By definition, this program is long term, implemented for at least 6 years in Grades K–5, and high intensity, addressing all of the Prism Model dimensions, rather than only one or two as in other program types.

ESL pullout (Line 6) is the most commonly encountered program in the U.S. for English learners. At elementary school level students are pulled out of the mainstream classroom for their time with an ESL teacher, and this type of ESL is taught as a subject at secondary level. ESL content (Line 5) is taught at both elementary and secondary levels and among English-only programs is less common than ESL pullout. Transitional bilingual education (Lines 3 and 4) is the most common bilingual program type across the U.S. One-way and two-way dual language enrichment programs (Lines 1 and 2) are less common bilingual program types than transitional but expanding rapidly as more and more schools discover that this enrichment model is more effective. We also included in this figure a series of 2-year longitudinal looks at the results from California's Proposition 227 program approved by voters in 1998 (Line 7) to compare English learners' achievement in that state to other program types.

As can be seen in Figure 5.2, significant differences in student performance begin to appear as they leave their elementary school instruction and continue in the cognitively demanding secondary school years, with dramatic differences seen in student achievement by the end of their schooling. Yet when examined as a cumulative difference across 10 school years, the very large difference between Line 1 and Line 6 is an average of 3.7 NCEs per year. That is, students attending the two-way dual language program were able to gain 3–4 NCEs per year more than typical native English speakers in each school year, on average. In contrast, students attending ESL pullout gained an average of 0 NCEs per year over the 10 years, keeping pace with but not closing the initial achievement gap with native English speakers.

The lowest-achieving program, initiated with the California voter referendum Proposition 227, helped students make gains in the early grades where they kept pace with native English speakers, but has not closed the achievement gap since its inception in 1998. This is even lower achievement than ESL pullout. In the early grades only, all students in all program types except Proposition 227, are making greater gains than native English speakers and appear to be closing the achievement gap at least through Grades K–3 while they are attending the special program, but this progress does not continue as students reach upper elementary years and beyond. At middle school and high school years, Proposition 227 has resulted in even more disastrous consequences for ESL students, where the gap is widening significantly between native English speakers and English learners.

These achievement differences in the secondary school years, seen in Figure 5.2, can be clearly attributed to program type attended in elementary school, since we took great care to match student cohorts by socioeconomic status, first and second language proficiency, and amount of formal schooling, with all students in this longitudinal picture having received all their schooling in the U.S. Our multiple regression analyses on the influence of other student background variables indicated that the program model variable had by far the strongest effect on student achievement, after socioeconomic status and first language proficiency were controlled. The research term "controlled" means that we limited the analyses presented in Figure 5.2 to only students with low socioeconomic status (on free and reduced lunch) and students who started school with no proficiency in English.

In Figure 5.2, the dotted flat line at the 50th percentile or normal curve equivalent (NCE–an equal-interval percentile) across Grades K–12 represents typical native English speakers' performance on these tests. These students are making 10 months of progress with each 10-month year of school. This is the national comparison group with whom English learners are competing as they move through the school years. Our goal as educators is that students just beginning development of the English language, who therefore start school not on grade level in English (where grade level is defined as the 50th NCE on the tests in English), will as a group eventually reach the 50th NCE and be able to sustain that general level of achievement during the rest of their school years.

In this figure, when a line is going up toward the 50th percentile/NCE, that means that English learners are making more than 1 year's progress with each year of school, gradually closing the achievement gap with native English speakers. When English learners as a group reach the 50th NCE (the flat, dotted line representing typical native English speakers making 1 year's progress in 1 year's time), they have as a group completely closed the achievement gap when tested in English. There will always be some high and some low scorers in every group of students, and half of each group will always be above and half below the group average. But the goal is for no large groups of students to be scoring significantly lower than the 50th percentile/NCE. This figure clearly demonstrates that it takes an average of 6 years to reach grade-level achievement in second language when starting at the 20th NCE (8th percentile), and that can only be achieved in programs that provide nonstop cognitive, academic, and linguistic support to allow students to accelerate their growth by an average 1½ years per year for 6 years in a row. The gap is closed at the average rate of 5 NCEs per year, with English learners outgaining the native English speakers by about one fourth of a national standard deviation per year. After 6 years of such gains, the full gap (1½ standard deviations or 30 NCEs) is closed. Not many special programs provide that kind of support for the English learner.

Program differences

To understand Figure 5.2, it is necessary to define some of the basic differences between programs. Figure 5.3 presents an overview of major U.S. program models developed for English learners, by identifying the major characteristics that distinguish one program from another.

This figure illustrates, in a continuum from left to right, the programs with the least amount of support to the programs with the most effective support. The program characteristics also parallel the dimensions of the Prism Model, presented in the previous chapter. This figure shows that programs such as Proposition 227 and ESL pullout that provide support in only one Prism dimension—learning the English language—are the least effective; whereas the most effective programs are dual language enrichment programs on the right side of the figure that provide support in all eight dimensions of the Prism—nonstop sociocultural, cognitive, academic, and linguistic development through both first and second languages. Furthermore, dual language programs provide this more effective support long enough for English learners to completely close the achievement gap in English, reaching grade-level achievement and staying there throughout the remainder of their schooling. Let us examine each of these programs in some detail, from least effective to most effective.

Proposition 227 in California. The referendum approved by California voters in 1998 specifies that students not proficient in English should be placed in a 1-year program to learn intensive English. This program segregates English learners in a classroom separate from the English mainstream. The referendum does not

Figure 5.3

Summary of Characteristics and Effectiveness of Common U.S. Programs for English Learners

	REMEDIAL					ENRICHMENT	
	As well implemented					As well implemented	
While in these programs students receive:	Proposition 227 in CA (as in law; not a program)	ESL Pullout	ESL Taught Through Content	TBE* with Traditional Teaching	TBE* with Current Teaching	One-way DL/DBE** — one group taught in two languages	Two-way DL/DBE** — two groups taught in their two languages
Cognitive Emphasis	None	Little	Some	Some	Moderate	Strong	Strong
Academic Emphasis (in all school subjects)	None	None	Yes	Yes	Yes	Yes	Yes
Linguistic Emphasis L1=primary lang, L2=English	Only Social English (only in L2)	Only Social English (only in L2)	Academic English (only in L2)	Develops Partial L1 + L2 Academic Proficiency	Develops Partial L1 + L2 Academic Proficiency	Develops Full L1 + L2 Academic Proficiency	Develops Full L1 + L2 Academic Proficiency
Sociocultural Emphasis C1=1st culture C2=2nd culture	None	Little	Some	Some	Moderate	Strong C1+C2	Strong C1+C2
Program Length	Transitory 1 year	Short-term 1-2 years	Short-term 2-3 years	Short-term 2-3 years	Intermediate 3-4 years	Sustained 6-12 years	Sustained 6-12 years
Native Language Academic Support	None	None	None	Some	Moderate	Strong	Strong
Exposure to English Speakers	No self-contained class	Yes in mainstream class	Yes half day after first year	No self-contained class	Yes Half-day	Yes Half-day	Yes All day
Extra Instructional Cost	High (extra teachers needed)	High (extra teachers needed)	High (extra teachers needed)	Small-to-moderate (special curriculum)	Small-to-moderate (special curriculum)	Least expensive: Standard mainstream curriculum	Least expensive: Standard mainstream curriculum
Percent of Achievement Gap With Native English Speakers Closed by End of Schooling (based on data-analytic research)	Unresearched longitudinally but no cross-sectional evidence of gap closure by ELLs since beginning in 1998	None final average scores at 11th national percentile (maximum is 18th)	Less than 50% final average scores at 22nd national percentile (maximum is 32nd)	Less than 50% final average scores at 24th national percentile	More than 50% final average scores at 32nd national percentile (but 90-10 TBE at 45th percentile)	100% of gap fully closed by end of school— average scores at or above 50th national percentile	100% of gap fully closed by end of school— average scores above 50th national percentile

* TBE stands for *transitional bilingual education*   ** DL/DBE stands for *dual language/ developmental bilingual education*

address how the students are to be given access to the rest of the curriculum—math, science, and social studies. But the main intent of the referendum is to deny students instruction through their first language—only English instruction is allowed. In the years following voter approval of the referendum, few schools in California have chosen to deny students access to the curriculum, but many have felt obligated to eliminate bilingual instruction. Only in schools where parents requested waivers have students been given continuing instruction through both their first language and English. Some schools chose to continue or develop two-way dual language programs as another alternative to the referendum, a program supported by English-speaking parents who choose for their children to participate in the bilingual enrichment classes. As a result of the voter referendum, only about 14% of English learners in California continue to be taught through two languages, as compared to about 29% of English learners receiving instruction in two languages prior to Proposition 227.

Proposition 227 as described in the referendum provides the least support for the eight dimensions of the Prism Model, supporting one dimension only, development of the English language (as seen in Figure 4.7). Sociocultural support is not addressed in this program. The teachers are expected to teach only in English and respond to students only in English. In these English classes, a bicultural curriculum that would address some of the affective aspects of learning is not encouraged. Cognitive development is not addressed in the language of the referendum. Since students are to be taught exclusively in English in a segregated context where they do not have access to native-English-speaking peers, there is little stimulus for cognitive development, which best occurs in interactions with same-age peers in second language, or through age-appropriate problem-solving tasks done in first language. Even academic development is ignored in this voter referendum, with heavy emphasis on English development, rather than teaching English through meaningful academic content.

The referendum also clearly dictates that all instruction will be in English, so students are denied four more dimensions of the Prism—access to linguistic, cognitive, academic, and sociocultural development through their primary language. And so, Proposition 227 addresses very few of the Prism Model components. As such, it can be described as a program weak in theoretical support. Its mechanisms and strategies for closing the achievement gap for English learners are few in number and weak in strength. It clearly fails the first of the three *Castañeda v. Pickard* (1981) tests (described in Chapter Two), since it is not based on sound educational theory.

How have students fared under Proposition 227? Regular news articles in the popular U.S. media herald the "large gains" made by English learners since

Proposition 227 was passed. Data analyses conducted by researchers have found that the general public is being misled by journalists' reports. It is to be expected that all groups of students will make gains with every year of school. The main point of school effectiveness research is to measure the gains of the norm group (native English speakers) and compare that to the gains of other groups doing less well in school. What the news articles don't tell the general public is that the native English speakers in California have tended to make more gains each year than English learners, and thus the gap between the two groups has actually widened since Proposition 227 began. And so, the "large gains" of English learners have been eclipsed by the even larger gains or normal progress of native English speakers, whose education was not impacted by Proposition 227.

Myhill (2004) and Collier & Thomas (2004) both found that the initial large achievement gap widened further in the early grades following the implementation of Proposition 227 in 1998. Other researchers analyzing California data found that the pre-Proposition 227 achievement gap remained large and unchanged by Proposition 227 (Parrish et al, 2006; Thompson, DiCerbo, Mahoney & MacSwan, 2002). No researchers performing gap closure analyses have found evidence of gap closure in the wake of Proposition 227.

In fact, when compared to other ELL programs, this program type has resulted in the lowest achievement for English learners of any program in the U.S. (Collier & Thomas, 2004). This achievement pattern can clearly be seen in Figure 5.2, line 7. We compared the performance of English learners attending Proposition 227 programs from Grade 2 to Grade 4, Grade 3 to Grade 5, and so on. These achievement lines should be going up, especially in the early grades. But they are relatively flat. That means no achievement gap closure is occurring for these students. Remember that to close the achievement gap, students have to make more than 1 year's gain for many years in a row. English learners in California are pacing the native English speakers, making 1 year's progress with each passing year, but not closing the gap. This means that they may eventually be denied access to higher education with these low scores, and many are likely to leave school in frustration before completing a high school degree.

Arizona passed a similar English-only measure, Proposition 203, and Massachusetts voters also approved such a measure. But English-only referenda in other states have not been approved by voters since 2003. Given the research findings to date from Proposition 227, it is not wise for other states to follow such programs, because they will suffer the consequences of low academic performance, and a large segment of the workforce will be underprepared for the workplace of the 21st century.

ESL pullout (elementary) or ESL taught as a subject (secondary). This is the most commonly encountered program for English learners in the U.S. When a school district receives their first students who don't speak English, ESL pullout is initially a natural choice for the first services provided by hiring an ESL teacher to serve as a resource teacher to support the students as they acquire English. Typically, as more English learners enroll in an elementary school, the ESL teacher assigned to that school receives students for 1 to 2 hours per day, pulling the students out of their mainstream classes for special support to learn the English language. At middle and high school level, English learners are assigned to ESL as one of their subjects for one or two classes per day.

There are substantial problems with this model, though. At elementary school level, usually ESL students from Grades K–5 are pulled out during different times of the day, so that at any given time the ESL teacher might have a mixture of ages in his/her class. Thus, one student in the pullout group might be missing science, another missing math, another social studies. The ESL teacher may do a great job working on English development, but does not have enough time to coordinate the missed academic lessons for each student. Moreover, the wide range of ages sometimes makes it difficult to provide the most meaningful cognitive and academic support while students are in the pullout ESL class. At secondary level, in first-, second-, and third-year ESL, the mainstream classes during the remainder of the day are not designed to meet second-language students' needs, so the students miss a lot of academic work while acquiring English. The result of this is predictable—an achievement gap with the constantly advancing native English speakers who are not subject to these limitations.

Examining the Prism Model dimensions, we find that ESL pullout or ESL as a subject, like Proposition 227, provides minimal support for English learners. The ESL teacher is not responsible for teaching academic subjects, and no support for development of academic skills through students' primary language is provided. Because the students are with the ESL teacher for relatively short periods of time, it is difficult to get into cognitively complex lessons, so cognitive development is not strongly supported. The main role of the ESL teacher is to teach the structure of the English language and to provide support for oral and written English language development. One other Prism dimension, sociocultural support, may be addressed while students are with the ESL teacher, but that is for a minimal amount of time. Program length for ESL pullout is minimal, generally 1 to 2 years, and amount of time per day with the ESL teacher is minimal at 1 to 2 hours per day (with only first-year ESL students getting more time with the ESL teacher). Thus, total student exposure to needed support services is quite limited overall.

Our research findings across numerous school districts in the U.S. indicate that the average achievement levels of high school graduates who were initially placed in ESL pullout programs is the 11th percentile (24th NCE) by the end of their school years. These students are therefore denied the opportunity to continue their schooling in higher education. Furthermore, the largest number of high school dropouts come from this program model (Thomas & Collier, 1997). Little or no long-term gap closure is associated with ESL pullout.

As can be seen in Figure 5.2, Line 6, students receiving ESL pullout in the early grades, K–3, are doing very well initially, closing the achievement gap by making more than 1 year's progress each year of school. By the time they are exited from their special support program, usually by second grade, it appears that they will do just fine in the rest of their education. As educators we wish them well and typically don't continue to follow them after they leave the ESL program. But as they move into the cognitively more challenging work at upper elementary grades and middle school, they may continue to make 1 year's progress in 1 year's time, but they are no longer closing the achievement gap in their mainstream classes. By the high school years, the effects of missed academic and cognitive development in the early grades begins to show up, as they still make good progress each year, but no longer are keeping pace with the native English speakers, who are always surging ahead academically. So in their high school years, former English learners who had attended ESL pullout are making perhaps 6 to 7 months' progress compared to the 10 months of progress of the native English speakers. Ultimately, by the last years of high school (if they haven't given up in frustration and left school), former English learners are back at the 11th percentile as a group by Grade 11 standards, having made 12 years of progress but never having permanently closed the achievement gap with their native-English peers.

ESL taught through academic content, also called sheltered instruction. This program takes ESL instruction one step further by adding academic content to the responsibilities of the ESL teacher (or an ESL teacher teaming with a content teacher), and adds two significant Prism components–academic and cognitive development in the second language, English. This program provides a very important step towards the kind of support needed to get students to a higher level of academic achievement. As can be seen in Figure 5.2, Line 5, we have found in our research studies that students receiving a quality ESL content program can close half of the achievement gap, graduating high school at the 22nd national percentile (34th NCE). This important finding has now been confirmed in two major national five-year studies (Thomas & Collier, 1997, 2002).

In an ESL content program, students accelerate their growth through lessons that teach English through meaningful academic content, and the ESL classes are cognitively more complex, an important dimension that is missing from ESL pull-out and Proposition 227 support services. In ESL content classes, sociocultural support can be provided, with teachers who understand the second language acquisition process, and aspects of bicultural curricular learning may be incorporated in the lessons. ESL content classes typically provide at least 1 more year of support than ESL pullout, so that the Prism dimensions supported by the ESL content teacher are extended for a longer period of time. This accelerates English learners' achievement for 1 more year before they move into the mainstream for the full school day, where gap closure generally ceases (although gains continue). Acceleration is needed for English learners to achieve gap closure, but English learners don't usually experience this in the mainstream. In order to accelerate their achievement, they must make more than 1 year's progress every year to catch up to the native English speaker who makes 1 year's progress every year.

An ESL content program may be taught by ESL teachers who are dual-certified to teach both ESL and the content areas, or the classes may be team-taught, with the content expert responsible for knowing the subject being taught and the amount of material to be covered and the ESL teacher responsible for making the content meaningful to students through second language techniques. When the demographics allow a large program to be developed, first-year beginning ESL students might be placed in ESL content classes all day, with lots of sociocultural and emotional support as well as English development. Second-year ESL students would then be integrated with team-taught mainstream classes for one or two subjects and other more difficult subject areas would continue to be taught in separate ESL content classes. Over a 3 to 4 year period, ESL students are gradually integrated with the English mainstream.

ESL content programs were expanded by many U.S. schools in the 1980s as the numbers of ESL students increased and schools realized that they were not meeting students' needs with only ESL pullout. However, ESL content graduates remain in the bottom quartile of students' achievement across the U.S., half-way to grade level, but still significantly below typical performance of native English speakers. These programs meet some of the students' needs for half of the Prism dimensions–sociocultural, cognitive, academic and linguistic support in English. But development of these dimensions through students' primary language is still missing.

The remaining program types in our list all provide some form of primary language support, and they have built on the teaching ideas developed in ESL content, so that ESL content serves as an important model for teaching language through academic content. Any bilingual program consists of ESL content for the English portion of the academic year, and it informs the teaching style that is used in the primary language instructional time as well. Thus, an effective ESL content program is a major part of all bilingual programs, which offer "English-Plus" in the form of ESL academic instruction plus first language academic instruction.

Transitional bilingual education. *Transitional bilingual education* is a commonly encountered program in the U.S., especially in the states with very large numbers of English learners of one language background, such as Spanish speakers. When state legislation for bilingual schooling has been provided, usually transitional bilingual education is the model chosen to receive state funding. This type of bilingual schooling is a *remedial* model, designed to move students into all-English instruction as soon as possible, but to provide some support for their academic learning through their first language. Transitional bilingual classes are generally offered for 2 to 3 years, after which English learners are moved into the mainstream with no more special support. In the transitional bilingual program, students continue (or begin) their academic and cognitive development in first language on grade level, while acquiring academic English. English learners receive first language instructional support in some subjects, combined with a portion of time in ESL content instruction. This program significantly increases the number of Prism dimensions addressed within the short duration of the transitional classes. Academic, cognitive, and linguistic development are provided through both English and students' primary language, in a socioculturally supportive environment, when the classes are well implemented.

Yet there are problems with this model that limit its effectiveness, when compared to more enriched forms of bilingual instruction. Transitional bilingual classes are usually self-contained, separate from the mainstream. They are frequently perceived by native-English-speaking students as remedial classes, designed for students who have "problems." The same is true for separate ESL classes. The low social status of students in the program can lead to subtle but powerful influences on English learners' academic achievement. English learners know that they are looked down upon and they can sense discriminatory behaviors towards them as they attend segregated ESL and bilingual classes. Social status relations tend to stay the same between majority and minority students with classes that segregate minority students.

What does this mean? While students may feel socioculturally supported within the classes, they sense lack of sociocultural support in the broader school context. Even when bilingual/bicultural teachers are warm and caring and supportive emotionally and cross-culturally, students become increasingly aware of their lower social status within the whole school community. Furthermore, the bilingual teachers often feel under pressure to switch to English as quickly as possible, reducing instructional time in the students' stronger and more instructionally efficient language and thus lessening the cognitive complexity of lessons. Students then perceive the switch to English as a message that their first language is not valued. Since first language is closely connected to identity, they come to view themselves as not worthy, not valued or respected for who they are. This leads to lower academic achievement in English in the long term.

Schools usually provide transitional bilingual (TBE) classes for only 2 to 3 years; this is referred to as *early-exit TBE*. By the end of their high school years, former English learners from this program have reached about the same level of achievement as those who received a high quality ESL content program, at the 24th national percentile (35th NCE), having closed half of the achievement gap. (See Figure 5.2, Line 4.) Some transitional bilingual classes have been able to improve the quality of the programs, by helping teachers utilize methods that encourage interactive, discovery learning, and by increasing the length of the program to 3 to 4 years. As seen in Figure 5.2, Line 3, student graduates of these classes reached the 32nd percentile (40th NCE).

Some TBE programs labeled *late-exit TBE* extend remedial services in primary language through the end of elementary school. Our analyses do not include this model, but if done more as an enrichment model, late-exit TBE has the potential to result in achievement closer to one-way dual language education. Overall, our research results from transitional bilingual programs demonstrate that students need more effective instructional support through their primary language for a longer time than that provided by most early-exit transitional bilingual classes, until they reach grade-level achievement in second language.

One-way and two-way dual language education. To avoid the negative social perceptions of transitional bilingual education, U.S. schools have worked on enriching their bilingual programs in well defined, research-supported ways, and they are increasingly using the term *dual language education* to refer to an enhanced, enriched, and more effective model of bilingual schooling. Dual language programs are qualitatively different from other bilingual programs. As many bilingual educators have experimented with variations in implementation, certain key characteristics have been validated by research. We will emphasize these validated models in this discussion.

While these programs were the least common model in U.S. schools a decade ago, they are rapidly increasing in number as educators discover the additional power of these programs to raise academic achievement for all students who choose to enroll. Dual language education is the curricular mainstream, taught through two languages. Students are educated together throughout the day in cognitively challenging, grade-level academic content in interactive classes that emphasize solving problems in authentic, real-world contexts. Alternating between the two languages takes place not by translation, but by subject or thematic unit or instructional time, so that after several years students become academically proficient in both languages of instruction, able to do academic work on grade level in either language. By attending this program, English learners can fully close the achievement gap in English, reaching high attainment, at or above the 50th percentile (grade-level achievement) in both their primary language and in English by the middle school years and graduating above grade level by the end of high school. (See Figure 5.2, Lines 1 and 2.)

The only difference between the two enrichment bilingual models, *one-way* and *two-way*, is the demographic mix of students who attend the bilingual classes. One-way refers to one language group being schooled through two languages. For example, Spanish speakers receive the mainstream academic curriculum through both English and Spanish. Two-way refers to two language groups being schooled through their two languages and thus teaching each other. Two-way classes include native English speakers who have chosen to be schooled bilingually, and their achievement is also typically at or above grade level when enrolled in these bilingual classes (Lindholm-Leary, 2001; Thomas & Collier, 2002). In two-way bilingual classes, the English learners are not segregated in a remedial program. Instead, they are respected and valued as learning partners. Furthermore, they are needed as important peer teachers when instruction is in their first language. Their English-speaking peers provide peer teaching support when the instruction is in English. The dual language teachers support both groups socioculturally through a bilingual/bicultural curriculum and provide a context for all students to develop cognitively, linguistically, and academically through both languages for at least 6 years all during the elementary school years (Grades K–5).

Many of these programs now continue into middle school and increasing numbers of high schools are developing courses in both languages, continuing the academic challenge beyond the elementary school years. If a school district has very few native English speakers, one-way enrichment dual language classes will get students to grade level in English by around eighth grade, the end of the middle school years. If a two-way enrichment dual language program provides the balance of native English speakers (one third to one half of the class) needed for peer teaching to stimulate cognitive, linguistic, and academic development, students reach grade level in second language usually by the end of the elementary school years in fifth grade, and sometimes sooner. These enrichment models of bilingual schooling address all of the Prism Model dimensions for at least 6 school years, allowing students to reach grade-level achievement in second language. These programs are capable of delivering potent instruction, higher test scores, and the kind of curricular reform needed to address the life and workplace needs of the 21st century.

In the next chapter, we shall explore some additional research findings and implications of these enrichment programs for education decision-making.

Analyzing your school and school district

Next steps to take: Now it's time to be realistic and examine what types of programs you actually have. Do the characteristics of each school's program match the name given to the program?

First, for English learners, what portion of the standard curriculum is provided through the students' primary language in their first year? For how many years is this academic work through primary language provided? Is yours an English-only program, providing ESL support? Have you improved the ESL instructional time by teaching ESL through academic content? If you have a bilingual program, have all the bilingual and ESL teachers been well trained in methods of teaching academic content through the second language? Use Figure 5.3 to answer these questions and classify your program.

Second, it's important to continue to analyze the needs of the English learners arriving in your school district. The arrival of large numbers of students usually requires a registration center with bilingual staff who can do the following: interview the family; conduct a home language survey; test students on their level of proficiency in English, and if possible, their academic achievement in primary language; assess amount of prior formal schooling; and decide on the age-appropriate grade level for each student. Older students who have missed a significant amount of formal schooling especially need extra support through first and second languages, which is sometimes provided in a newcomer school for their first year.

Do you have a registration center? Does the staff keep records by primary language, age on arrival, grade level assigned, amount of prior formal schooling, and the date each ESL learner began acquiring the English language? These statistics for the school district help all staff make decisions about the types of services needed and provide important data for longitudinal analyses of students' academic achievement over time.

Third, after examining your student statistics and program types, do you have the best programs to close the academic gap? What would you need to change to improve your services to English learners? If your school district did not "pass" the *Thomas-Collier Test* for all at-risk groups (described in Chapter 3 and Appendix B), can you visualize new ways of schooling all your students?

Fourth, the school board of course wants to save money. Any existing separate programs in your school district that add on to the curricular mainstream tend to cost a lot more, because you are adding extra resource staff, and salaries for staff are the most expensive item in a school budget. Could you consider an enrichment dual language model instead of your existing programs? This is the most cost-effective program, because the student-teacher ratio is the same as that of the standard curriculum. In dual language, when two teachers team-teach two classes, the existing student-teacher ratio is maintained and staffing for the program is not more costly than the standard. Also, a bilingual teacher deeply proficient in both languages can serve as the instructional leader for both languages.

What additional expenditures are essential for converting a remedial bilingual instructional approach to an enrichment dual language approach? In your planning year, have you included visits to high quality dual language schools? Have you planned for ongoing staff development as well as dual language training sponsored by local, state, or national organizations? Does the budget include choosing quality instructional materials in the first and second languages? Have you provided for ongoing leadership support? Are there funds for development of promotional materials to explain the program to the community? This program will save instructional costs, and yet a portion of those savings must be reallocated to the dual language program to provide for valid program implementation and to allow the program to reach its full potential.

Dual language education works exceedingly well for all students, including native English speakers, linguistically diverse students who are fluent in English, and all at-risk groups. All students can work together in an instructionally rich context.

REFLECTIONS FROM THE FIELD

Highland Forest Elementary, in the East Central Independent School District located in San Antonio, Texas, has been implementing a very successful 90:10 two-way dual language program for 8 years. Based on the program's success and the demand by parents and community, the superintendent approved all elementary and secondary schools' implementation of the 90:10 two-way dual language program with set dual language guidelines. As the program is phased in to the new schools and grade levels, school staff, parents, and students are presented with the research findings and program best practices of Dr. Virginia Collier and Dr. Wayne Thomas.

Every year as the students take the TAKS (Texas Assessment of Knowledge & Skills), students participating in the Two-Way Dual Language Program are consistently the highest achieving students in the district. The 90:10 Two-Way Immersion program, in our opinion, should be the standard program for all students in the United States. Our children deserve a well-rounded education where multilingualism is the standard. As language educators, we need to advocate for multilingualism as the "way of the future."

IRIS GONZÁLEZ-ORNELAS, BILINGUAL/ESL COORDINATOR
MANUEL E. ORNELAS, PRINCIPAL
LEGACY MIDDLE SCHOOL
EAST CENTRAL ISD, SAN ANTONIO, TEXAS

CHAPTER SIX: ENRICHMENT PROGRAMS AND POLICY IMPLICATIONS

In the first section of this chapter, we clarify some of the misinformation that is present in the U.S. media reports on our field. Educators not familiar with the field of bilingual/ESL education need to know basic program variations, in addition to the general program models defined in the previous chapter. Thus in the following paragraphs we will discuss the terms *immersion*, *90:10 bilingual immersion*, *structured English immersion*, and then we will illustrate student achievement in both the 90:10 and 50:50 dual language models. Later in this chapter we will discuss research results from *submersion* when parents refused special bilingual/ESL support services for their children, and other research results that demonstrate the importance of primary language schooling for English learners.

Clarifying some confusing program names in the research on program effectiveness

A form of enrichment dual language education that has become popular in some schools in the southwest U.S. is the 90:10 model. This type of program was originally named **immersion** in Canada in the 1960s. It was developed for language majority students (native English speakers) to receive their schooling through two languages—French and English—throughout their schooling, Grades K–12. The term immersion meant that students would be *immersed* 90% of the instructional time during Grades K–1 in a *minority language*—not English—followed by intensive academic work through both the minority and majority language through the remainder of the school years.

As this model is being increasingly adopted in the U.S., it has become known as the **90:10 bilingual immersion** model, or **90:10 dual language education**, implemented in most U.S. schools as a two-way program. It requires the strongest long-term commitment to academic development of the minority language along with the majority language. The 90:10 model requires initial emphasis on the minority language (for example, Spanish), because this language is less supported by the broader society, and thus academic uses of this language are less easily acquired outside of school. In this model, for Grades PK–1, 90% of the instructional time is conducted in the minority language and only 10% in English. Beginning with Grade 2, the instructional time in English is increased to 20%, until by Grade 4 (or sometimes Grade 5), academic instruction is presented equally in each language.

By Grade 6, the beginning of the middle school years, students have generally developed deep academic proficiency in both languages and they can work on math, science, social studies, and language arts at or above grade level in either language. In a 90:10 model, students continue their bilingual schooling into the middle and high school years, receiving some subjects in English and other subjects taught in the minority language. In research studies on this model, in both Canada and the U.S., academic achievement is very high for all groups of students participating in the program, when compared to comparable groups receiving schooling only through English (Cloud, Genesee & Hamayan, 2000; Cummins, 2000; Cummins & Swain, 1986; Dolson & Lindholm-Leary, 1995; Genesee, 1987; Lambert, 1984; Lindholm-Leary, 1990, 1991, 2001; Lindholm-Leary & Aclan, 1991; Thomas & Collier, 2002).

To avoid confusion, it is important to understand the distinction between immersion education in Canada, and the program model labeled *structured English immersion*, which has become the common name for programs described in the English-only laws being passed by voters in California, Arizona, and Massachusetts. Immersion educators in Canada developed immersion to be the strongest form of bilingual education, providing a full commitment to schooling in two languages throughout Grades K–12. The promoters of structured English immersion misinform educators when they state that it is based on the Canadian model. **In fact, structured immersion is the reverse of the Canadian model**, with no instructional support for the minority language and all instruction only in English, the majority language. At best, structured English immersion as it has been implemented in the U.S. is just another form of content ESL, taught in a self-contained classroom, with instruction all in English. At worst, it resembles ESL pullout, as a form of low-intensity English-only instruction. In the voters' referenda, students are given only 1 year of support in a structured English immersion class, followed by all instruction in the mainstream. This results in an extremely weak form of ESL content support because it is not provided for long enough to assist with closing some of the achievement gap. In Figures 5.2 and 5.3 in the previous chapter, we labeled this model *Proposition 227* so that it would not be confused with the stronger form of ESL content that provides support for 2 to 3 years.

It is very important for U.S. school policy makers to understand this misuse of the term immersion, because the popular media in the U.S. have misinformed the public on the research base for structured English immersion. Publications and press releases written by members of the English-only movement have stated that there are many research studies that show that students do very well in immersion programs. But the studies they are citing are the 90:10 immersion research studies from Canada and the U.S., describing bilingual programs that are entirely different from the English immersion experience that the English-only movement supports. In fact, the few studies actually conducted on structured English immersion found that this program in the long term leads to lower achievement than ESL pullout

(Collier, 1992). Even though structured English immersion is a self-contained ESL content class (with potentially higher achievement than ESL pullout), in the voters' referenda of California, Arizona, and Massachusetts, it is proposed that this program be provided for only 1 year and therefore provides even less support than the minimal support of ESL pullout.

Student achievement in 90:10 and 50:50 dual language programs

Let us briefly revisit from the previous chapter the academic achievement of English learners who have been placed in Proposition 227 programs (incorrectly labeled *immersion* by journalists in the popular U.S. media). As was seen in Figure 5.2, Proposition 227 has resulted in no gap closure. To date, it has the lowest achievement levels of any English learner program in the U.S. In contrast, the highest achievement occurs in 90:10 bilingual classes that emphasize strong academic and cognitive development in the minority language first, followed by increasing academic development in English, until the two languages are given equal instructional time. One example is the 90:10 program in Houston Independent School District (HISD),

implemented in both two-way and one-way schools. The following Figures 6.1 and 6.2 from our 2002 national research report (Thomas & Collier, 2002) illustrate HISD student achievement in Spanish and in English on the national norm-referenced tests.

Students in the two-way classes are above grade level in both languages through Grade 5. These students are mostly of low socioeconomic background, as measured by free or reduced lunch, growing up in the inner city. Despite this, they are flourishing academically in school in English as well as in Spanish, even though English was not emphasized until they reached the upper elementary grades.

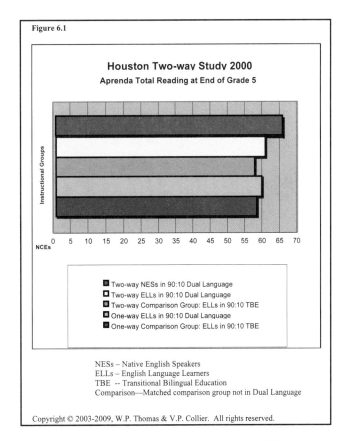

Figure 6.1

Houston Two-way Study 2000
Aprenda Total Reading at End of Grade 5

Instructional Groups

NCEs   0   5   10 15 20 25 30 35 40 45 50 55 60 65 70

■ Two-way NESs in 90:10 Dual Language
□ Two-way ELLs in 90:10 Dual Language
■ Two-way Comparison Group: ELLs in 90:10 TBE
□ One-way ELLs in 90:10 Dual Language
■ One-way Comparison Group: ELLs in 90:10 TBE

NESs – Native English Speakers
ELLs – English Language Learners
TBE -- Transitional Bilingual Education
Comparison—Matched comparison group not in Dual Language

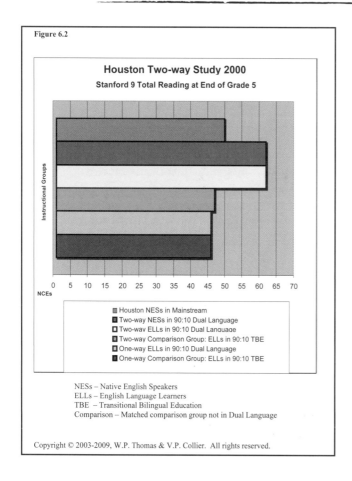

Figure 6.2

Houston Two-way Study 2000
Stanford 9 Total Reading at End of Grade 5

Instructional Groups

0 5 10 15 20 25 30 35 40 45 50 55 60 65 70
NCEs

- Houston NESs in Mainstream
- Two-way NESs in 90:10 Dual Language
- Two-way ELLs in 90:10 Dual Language
- Two-way Comparison Group: ELLs in 90:10 TBE
- One-way ELLs in 90:10 Dual Language
- One-way Comparison Group: ELLs in 90:10 TBE

NESs – Native English Speakers
ELLs – English Language Learners
TBE – Transitional Bilingual Education
Comparison – Matched comparison group not in Dual Language

Students also do exceedingly well in 50:50 models of enrichment dual language schooling, scoring at or above grade level in English, their second language. A 50:50 program teaches the mainstream curriculum through two languages, alternating half of the instructional time between the two languages. As seen in Figure 5.2, English learners in two-way 50:50 bilingual classes that lasted through the end of elementary school made it to grade level in English by sixth grade and had reached the 61st NCE (70th percentile) by the end of high school. English learners in one-way 50:50 bilingual classes, with no native English speakers attending their school, made it to grade level in English by eighth grade and were achieving at the 52nd NCE (54th percentile) when they graduated from high school.

An example from our national research report published in 2002 (Thomas & Collier, 2002) demonstrates the power of this program for schooling linguistically diverse students who are English-dominant. We collected data from two school districts in northern Maine whose Franco-American students were losing their heritage language, French. Their parents had been punished for speaking their language at school, and they viewed their French dialect as a street language not worthy of passing on to their children. But these rural communities were suffering economically, and they faced the possibility that their children as adults would have no means of employment and would have to leave the region to support themselves. Some of the school board members decided to experiment with acquisition of French in school as a means of economic revitalization for the towns, so that their children could develop businesses that would attract the French-speaking Canadians across the border. They had heard of Canadian immersion programs, and initially planned a 90:10 French-English program, but in implementation practices, the program became a 50:50 model. Within 4 years, the two comparison groups, initially similar before the start of the program, were significantly different in academic achievement. (See Figure 6.3.)

At the end of 4 years of schooling through two languages, the bilingually schooled students were outperforming their monolingually schooled counterparts by 15 NCEs (almost three fourths of a national standard deviation), even though they received only half a day of instruction in English, while their counterparts received a full day of English. The bilingually schooled students reached the 62nd NCE (71st percentile) in their strongest language, English, whereas before the program started they were achieving at the 40th NCE (32nd percentile) in English. This and many other studies on bilingual schooling demonstrate the intellectual stimulus for all children that comes from doing academic work through two languages. The cognitive advantages accelerate students' academic success, so that they make more than 1 year's gain within 1 school year. Many studies of children raised bilingually have found that proficient bilinguals are better at problem solving, creativity, and divergent thinking than monolinguals (Baker, 2006, 2007; Bialystok, 1991, 2001; Díaz & Klingler, 1991; Tokuhama-Espinosa, 2000, 2003), and the research on dual language schooling lends support to these findings.

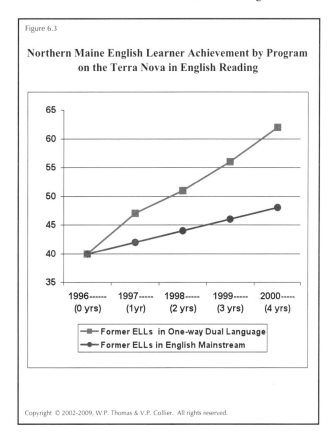

Figure 6.3

Northern Maine English Learner Achievement by Program on the Terra Nova in English Reading

Former ELLs in One-way Dual Language
Former ELLs in English Mainstream

When a school reaches decisions regarding which dual language program model to choose, many school administrators want to have an answer to the question of which program is "better." When comparing these variations in dual language, analyzing data across many school districts for annual gap closure and annual effect size, we found that overall, two-way 90:10 is the most efficient in closing the

Figure 6.4

Achievement Gap Closure For English Learners in Dual Language Programs— What Can We Expect?

Program Type	Annual Gap Closure	Annual Effect Size	% of Gap Closed by Grade 5
One-way 90:10	3 - 5 NCEs	0.14 - 0.24*	**70% - 100% +**
One-way 50:50	3 NCEs	0.14	**70%**
Two-way 90:10	4 - 6 NCEs	0.19 - .29*	**95%- 100% +**
Two-way 50:50	3.5 - 5 NCEs	0.17 - 0.24*	**70% - 100% +**

* = meaningful and significant annual effect

Notes:

1. Using norm-referenced tests—a difficult test measures the true gap size; an easier test underestimates the gap.
2. ELLs started at grade K with no exposure to English.
3. Achievement gap = 1.2-1.3 national standard deviations.
4. Statistically conservative effect sizes use unrestricted national standard deviations.

second language achievement gap in the shortest amount of time, with 95–100% of the gap closed by Grade 5. (See Figure 6.4.)

One-way 90:10 and two-way 50:50 are next in the power of program models, with 70–100% of the gap closed by Grade 5. One-way 50:50 requires continuing the program into the middle school years to ensure full gap closure. Yet all four of these program variations are the premier models for assisting students to reach the highest academic success. Why? Because all four have much higher long-term achievement outcomes than remedial bilingual or remedial ESL-only programs.

In summary, enrichment 90:10 and 50:50 one-way and two-way dual language programs are the only programs we and other researchers have found to date that assist English learners to fully reach the 50th percentile (grade-level) in English and to maintain that level of high achievement—or reach even higher levels—by the end of high school. Also, the fewest dropouts come from these programs. An additional benefit is that these students also achieve grade-level performance in their first language, graduating deeply proficient in two languages. Thus, they are resources for the community, the professional world, and the larger society, able to make use of their two languages as adults for the benefit of the communities of the 21st century.

Does submersion in the English mainstream work better?

Although *Lau v. Nichols* (1974) requires that all U.S. schools provide some kind of support program for English learners to make their education "meaningful," it is an interesting question that might prompt policy makers to ask–why not just submerse them in the English mainstream? Of course that's what our schools did in the first half of the 20th century, and there were few immigrants who managed to graduate from high school. In fact, only 20% of the total U.S. population graduated from high school as of 1940. How times have changed! Despite the plea that "my Uncle George did just fine and he didn't get any special help," Uncle George did not need to graduate from high school to be successful. Furthermore, most new immigrants of the early 20th century did not learn English because they did not need it to survive. It was the second and third generation immigrants to the U.S. who had to work on learning English to make a living.

We now have an answer for this interesting question–what would happen if you just submersed English learners in the English mainstream with no special support? Even though the Supreme Court ruling of *Lau v. Nichols* requires a support program, parents can choose what type of schooling they want for their children. So in any large school system, it is possible to have a significant number of students placed in whatever program the parents request. In Houston Independent School District (HISD), one of our research sites with over 210,000 students, we and HISD staff found 1,599 English learners whose parents had refused bilingual and ESL services, saying that they wanted their children to be placed in a mainstream English class. The school staff had strongly counseled the parents that this was not a wise decision, but ultimately it was the parents' choice. This situation gave us an opportunity as researchers to find out how these students did as they reached the end of high school, and the results are not a happy picture. (See Figure 6.5.)

Initially, when first tested in English at second grade, these English learners were performing on grade level, so it would be natural for parents to assume they had made the right decision. But by fourth grade, these students' scores were at the 34th NCE (22nd percentile), and by middle school years, significant numbers of these students were leaving without completing their high school degree.

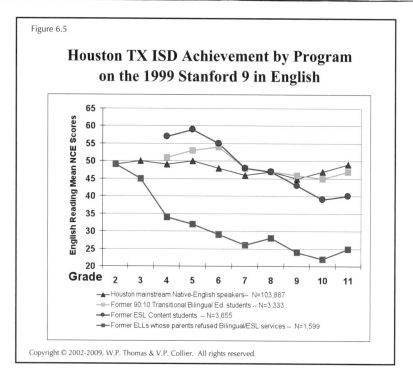

Figure 6.5

Houston TX ISD Achievement by Program on the 1999 Stanford 9 in English

English Reading Mean NCE Scores

Grade

—▲— Houston mainstream Native-English speakers-- N=103,887
—■— Former 90:10 Transitional Bilingual Ed. students -- N=3,333
—●— Former ESL Content students -- N=3,655
—■— Former ELLs whose parents refused Bilingual/ESL services -- N=1,599

Those remaining in tenth grade were scoring at the 22nd NCE (9th percentile), and after many more dropped out of school, the few remaining eleventh graders were at the 25th NCE (12th percentile).

We then decided to compare the achievement of English learners receiving no special program to the achievement levels of English learners in the next lowest achieving program, Proposition 227. Our intent was to determine how much more the students in California were benefitting from at least 1 year of a special support program. Shockingly, English learners in Proposition 227 programs are similar in achievement on the same national test to the English learners in Houston schools who were submersed in the English mainstream with no special program at all, as seen in Figure 6.6.

Apparently, 1 year of support followed by placement in the English mainstream has about the same achievement outcome as no support at all. The "great gains" for English learners under California's Proposition 227 reported in the popular press do not match the greater, normal gains that native English speakers make each year, and so the gap between these two groups is widening with each school year. Other states should examine closely this gap closure issue. They need not make this serious mistake, leading to significant under-education of a large percentage of the school-age population.

We recommend that parents who refuse bilingual/ESL services for their children be informed that their children's long-term academic achievement will probably be much lower as a result. These parents should be strongly counseled against refusing bilingual/ESL services when their child is eligible. The research findings of this and many other studies indicate that

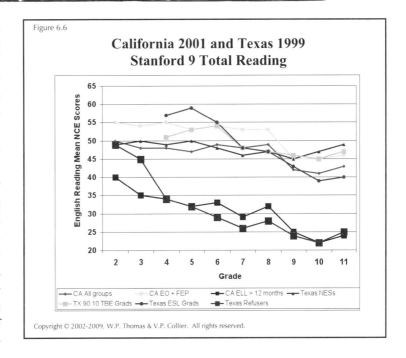

Figure 6.6

California 2001 and Texas 1999 Stanford 9 Total Reading

bilingual/ESL services, as required by *Lau v. Nichols*, raise students' achievement levels by significant amounts.

ESL content vs. transitional bilingual education

A next logical question to ask might be "why provide first language support?" Maybe providing more years of a quality ESL content program is the answer. Our data from Houston school district and from District E in the southeast U.S. (Thomas & Collier, 2002) help to answer this question. Figure 6.7 compares two groups of students in Houston schools who initially started school in kindergarten with no proficiency in English.

The English learners who received the ESL content program with no instruction in their first language were students of mostly Asian language background, with Chinese and Urdu speakers the largest language groups. Texas state laws mandate that bilingual instruction be provided for English learners in Grades PK–5 whose home language is spoken by 20 or more students in a single grade in a school. These Asian students received ESL content support for 4 to 5 years, rather than bilingual instruction, because they were too few in number for the school district to provide academic work taught through their first languages. The blue line shows the achievement of these students instructed only in ESL content. The green line represents English learners who were Spanish speakers and who received a late-exit transitional bilingual program with half a day in Spanish content and half a day in ESL content instruction for 4 to 5 years.

When the two groups were first tested in English on the norm-referenced test across the curriculum in fourth grade, both groups were achieving at or above grade level. However, the English learners schooled through ESL content were initially outperforming their counterparts schooled in Spanish/English bilingual classes in both fourth and fifth grades. Examining the short-term data (Grades PK–5), it would be natural for an elementary school principal to conclude at the end of fifth grade that the ESL content program worked better than transitional bilingual classes. But during the middle school years when instructional difficulty increased, both groups scored at similar levels on the Stanford 9. And the cognitive demand of instruction continues to increase into the high school years. It wasn't until ninth grade that the Hispanic students exited from bilingual programs began to outperform the Asian ESL content graduates, but by eleventh grade, the bilingually-schooled students were significantly higher in achievement at the 47th NCE (45th percentile), while those schooled all in English with a good ESL content program—for more years than most ESL programs—were at the 40th NCE (32nd percentile).

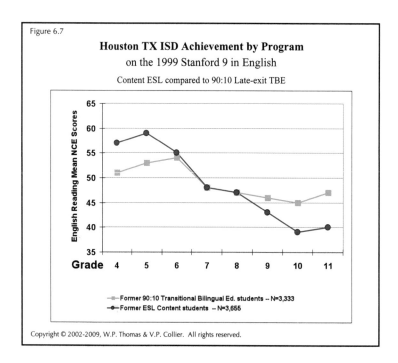

Figure 6.7

Houston TX ISD Achievement by Program
on the 1999 Stanford 9 in English

Content ESL compared to 90:10 Late-exit TBE

English Reading Mean NCE Scores

Former 90:10 Transitional Bilingual Ed. students -- N=3,333
Former ESL Content students -- N=3,655

Cognitive and academic slowdown occurred for the ESL content students schooled only in English, but it didn't show up in test scores until the high school years. Whereas having been schooled through two languages, the Spanish speakers did not get behind in school while they were learning English. The cognitive and academic advantage of this schooling through their first language is finally realized in test scores during the high school years, when the academic challenge is greatest and when the tests are most difficult.

One more example from District E demonstrates the difficulty of reaching higher levels of achievement, and fully closing the achievement gap, when schooling is all in English. This district has an outstanding ESL content program. We analyzed their longitudinal data, assuming that students would reach grade level in English after a number of years of good schooling. Their ESL content program had an average of 10 students per ESL teacher, well trained teachers fully certified in ESL and the content areas they were teaching, lots of sociocultural support for the students, respect for students' first languages and cultures, interactive discovery classes taught with cooperative learning strategies,

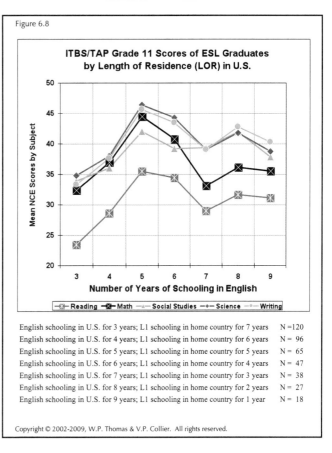

Figure 6.8

ITBS/TAP Grade 11 Scores of ESL Graduates by Length of Residence (LOR) in U.S.

English schooling in U.S. for 3 years; L1 schooling in home country for 7 years   N =120
English schooling in U.S. for 4 years; L1 schooling in home country for 6 years   N = 96
English schooling in U.S. for 5 years; L1 schooling in home country for 5 years   N = 65
English schooling in U.S. for 6 years; L1 schooling in home country for 4 years   N = 47
English schooling in U.S. for 7 years; L1 schooling in home country for 3 years   N = 38
English schooling in U.S. for 8 years; L1 schooling in home country for 2 years   N = 27
English schooling in U.S. for 9 years; L1 schooling in home country for 1 year   N = 18

and students remained in the ESL content program for 3 to 4 years for extra support. In other words, District E's ESL content program is "as good as it gets" for English-only instruction. Figure 6.8 illustrates that the highest level these English learners were able to reach on the standardized test in reading was the 36th NCE (26th percentile) by the end of high school.

In our analyses, we included only those students who were immigrants of many different language backgrounds and who arrived in the U.S. on grade level, having received grade-level formal schooling in their home countries before they emigrated here. But after 5 years of schooling in English, beginning with strong support in their ESL content program, they were only able to close half of the achievement gap with native English speakers and more years of schooling in English did not help them reach higher levels of achievement. As can be seen in Figure 6.8, those students with 7 to 9 years of schooling in the U.S. and 1 to 3 years of schooling in their home countries were achieving below the levels of those who received 5 years of schooling in the U.S. and 5 years of first language schooling in their home country.

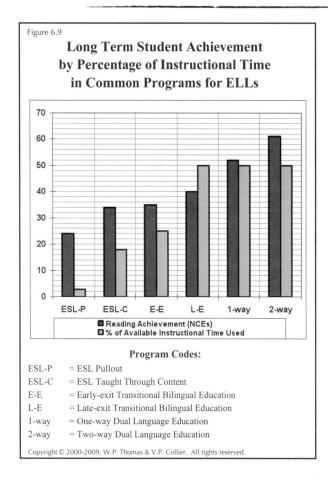

Figure 6.9

Long Term Student Achievement by Percentage of Instructional Time in Common Programs for ELLs

■ Reading Achievement (NCEs)
□ % of Available Instructional Time Used

Program Codes:

ESL-P = ESL Pullout
ESL-C = ESL Taught Through Content
E-E = Early-exit Transitional Bilingual Education
L-E = Late-exit Transitional Bilingual Education
1-way = One-way Dual Language Education
2-way = Two-way Dual Language Education

Amount of time in the bilingual/ESL program

Another way of looking at all of this data is to compare programs by the percentage of instructional time that students receive in the program. As can be seen in Figure 6.9, the amount of instructional support that each special program provides has a direct relationship to students' academic achievement in the long term.

The more instructional assistance in both first and second languages provided by qualified bilingual/ESL teachers, the higher English learners' achievement by the end of high school.

Influence of socioeconomic status on English learners' academic achievement

It is important that educators realize the true influence of students' socioeconomic status (SES) on English learners' achievement. Although SES is widely acknowledged as an important predictor of student success in school, many educators do not realize that there are other more important predictors. The negative effects of low SES can be reversed by other factors (Thomas & Collier, 2002). Those who believe that SES negatively affects achievement and is resistant to influence from schools might be tempted to select a minimal program for English learners, on the theory that SES influences achievement more than the school program.

Our analyses show that SES, considered separately, explains from 14 to 20% of English learners' achievement, depending on the test used. At first glance, this appears to confirm the notion that "they come from poor home backgrounds so what can we do?" But when the shared effects of other variables are statistically removed, the unique effect of SES is much smaller. In particular, a strong, effective program can reduce the negative effect of SES to less than 5%. (See Figure 6.10.)

We have found that the choice of program for English learners is more important than SES. An instructionally weak program, such as California's Proposition 227 or ESL pullout, allows SES to exert its full negative effect of 14 to 20%. However, for dual language programs, the unique effects of SES are reduced to less than 5%. Thus, it is especially important that educators choose powerful programs for English learners, since many English learners are from low SES backgrounds. Educators cannot change students' SES, but we can change the school program.

Conclusions

In summary, our longitudinal research findings demonstrate that the highest quality ESL content programs close about half of the total achievement gap. When English learners exit into the English mainstream, those schooled all in English initially may outperform those schooled bilingually when tested in English, but later, during the high school years, the bilingually-schooled students outperform the monolingually-schooled students. Students who receive at least 5 to 6 years of dual language schooling in the U.S. reach the 50th NCE/percentile in English by fifth to eighth grade and maintain that level of performance because they

Figure 6.10

Does Socio-economic Status (SES) Matter in Programs for English Learners?

Answer: Yes, but not as you may think it does.

When ineffective, weak programs are chosen in a school district, SES explains about 18% of ELL achievement and low SES exerts a potentially substantial negative effect.

But when well-implemented dual language programs are used instead, the negative effect of SES on ELL achievement is greatly reduced to less than 5%.

Conclusion: Strong, effective dual language programs can overcome or reverse much of the negative effect of low SES on achievement. Thus, educators should strongly consider dual language programs in low-SES instructional contexts for ELLs, and for other students as well.

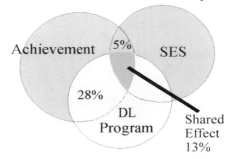

The Effect of Multicollinearity

have not lost any years of schooling. Students who are raised in a dual language environment need a minimum of 5 years of schooling in their first language and 5 years of schooling in their second language to achieve on grade level in either of the two languages. Providing bilingual schooling in the U.S. meets both needs simultaneously and leads to high academic achievement in the long term.

Bilingual/ESL content programs must be effective (gains must be at least 3–4 NCEs per year more than mainstream students are gaining per year), well implemented, not segregated, and sustained long enough (5 to 6 years) for the typical 25–30 NCE achievement gap between English learners and native English speakers to be closed. Even the most effective programs can only close half of the achievement gap in 2 to 3 years, the typical length of remedial programs for English learners. Therefore, short-term, remedial, and ineffective programs cannot close the large achievement gap and should be avoided, especially as educators move to close achievement gaps as required by the *No Child Left Behind* legislation.

An effective enrichment bilingual/ESL program must meet students' developmental needs. All students need a learning environment that provides nonstop support for linguistic (both first and second languages), academic, cognitive, emotional, social, and physical development. Schools need to create a natural learning environment that allows students to make progress in ways that are meaningful to them. To do this, classes must include an abundance of natural, rich oral and written language used by students and teachers. In bilingual classes, students' first and second languages are used in separate instructional contexts, not using translation. All students work together, doing meaningful, "real-world" problem-solving, in a media-rich environment with video, computers, and print. Challenging thematic units get and hold students' interests, using students' bilingual-bicultural knowledge to bridge to new knowledge across the curriculum. We can create a bilingual-bicultural school context for all our students that meets students' developmental needs through interaction with educated adults and includes sociocultural acceptance among student peers and staff, adequate nutrition, and a safe school environment.

Analyzing your school and school district

As your school or district considers the implementation or development of enrichment bilingual/ESL programs, take the time to think about your program options, student population and community context, and the many ramifications of these decisions.

Scenario: End of staff development retreat for central administration, principals, and school board members

Superintendent: *Okay, we've got our work cut out for us. Those research figures may have implications for us. What do you think?*

Elementary school principal: *Go back to Figure 5.2. I don't know about you guys, but my school's down here (line 6) and I want to be up here (line 1)! I need a lot more information about that kind of program, though.*

Another principal: *We can do it—let's go visit that school doing dual language that we've heard about in the neighboring county. That'd be a start, at least.*

Another principal: *Before we do that, do we know how their students are doing? Do we even know if their student population is similar to ours?*

School board member: *Have our parents been informed about those Houston results with kids whose parents refused bilingual/ESL services? We could be sued, you know. When new families register, they've got to be counseled using that research figure.*

District administrator: *I'd like clarification on our program. Do we have a clear statement in writing as to our policies? Do we really have a good quality ESL content program, or is it this weaker form of structured English immersion? What are our bilingual classes really like?*

Another school board member: *Wait a minute! Am I the only one here who doesn't even know what all those terms mean?*

High school principal: *I agree that we need to get clear on our plan for all students in all grades, PK–12. My feeder schools include many kids who have attended bilingual classes, and they don't get any meaningful continuation of courses in Spanish at my school. I've been thinking about this for awhile and we have enough students who have had academic work in Spanish in their elementary school to offer content courses in Spanish for credit. Why not do this in our middle schools and in my high school? I would need to think about staffing ...*

Superintendent: *We have a lot to think about and learn before we plan our next steps. Remember we are doing this to find a better approach to serve all of our students well, and realistically, it's going to take time. Ana (bilingual/ESL director), could we meet to identify some resources that might help us?*

Arrey Elementary School began its dual language program in 2006, starting with their kindergarten class and rolling up a class each year thereafter. We started the program primarily because the majority of our students came from Spanish-speaking homes. While the students spoke Spanish, they were not literate in their home language. At the same time, we found that students who had previous schooling in Mexico and were able to read and write in their native language were able to pick up the English language much, much faster. And, while the academic process of reading and writing takes a little longer, we are finding our students are making gains in both languages.

At Arrey Elementary, we are truly "pioneers" in that we are the only school in the district that has a dual language program ...

SUSAN TAYLOR, PRINCIPAL
ARREY ELEMENTARY SCHOOL
TRUTH OR CONSEQUENCES
MUNICIPAL SCHOOL DISTRICT
ARREY, NEW MEXICO

REFLECTIONS FROM THE FIELD

In 2005, we graduated our first class of dual language students— eight young men crossed through the portal to receive their high school diploma embossed with a dual language honor seal. Since then, two have earned university diplomas, and one has begun a Masters program in international business. In 2006, 14 students followed their trail, broadening the path. And in 2009, 64 dual language students graduated from three Ysleta high schools! The path is indelibly laid, the portal is open, and there is no turning back. Our dual language graduates are now present in growing numbers in our universities, military, and workforce, forever changing their lives and ours as they continue to lead and serve. They are emboldened, empowered, and equipped by an educational experience characterized by high expectations for biliteracy, cultural competence, and service.

Drs. Collier and Thomas write about the "Astounding Effectiveness of Dual Language Education for All," and what I have been privileged to witness is not merely an effective education for all students, but a truly transformational one. Dual language education, K–12, cultivates each individual's greatest human potential and guides him or her in molding it, adapting it, wielding it, and giving it voice to create a future that will astound us all.

CINDY SIZEMORE
YSLETA INDEPENDENT SCHOOL DISTRICT
EL PASO, TEXAS

CHAPTER SEVEN: VISUALIZING FUTURE SCHOOLS

Now here's the fun part! As you, the reader, envision what transformations can take place in our schools, you get to play with possibilities. Dream your dreams. Maybe those dreams can become reality. We don't have to stay stuck in the experiences of the past. Some visions may include past moments of wisdom and creativity that you have experienced in your life. Others may include special current happenings that have kernels of genius. Whatever mix of old and new ways of schooling that we want to create, if we keep in mind the principles that, according to the research cited throughout this book, make a difference with diverse student populations, then we can create new and visionary schools.

This short book provides explanations from research findings for envisioning effective schools for all students, including those of diverse language background. There are no prescriptions and no easy answers for the constantly changing needs of those who arrive at our school door. But if we work together, educators and students and families and communities, we can create extraordinary experiences with learning, with dramatic absorption of new knowledge and expression of ever-expanding knowledge. Let's see what visualizations we might start with, by first identifying some key concepts that permeate effective bilingual schools.

Developing cognition

Nonstop development of cognition is clearly one of the major keys to academic success for all. Stimulating thinking at all levels, with every school experience being multi-layered, is a basic concept for all learning experiences. In the past several decades we have spent considerable time over-simplifying material for English learners, for students with special needs, for students from poverty, for students in inner-city classrooms. Breaking the curriculum down into its miniscule components, we have spent so much time in the step-by-step details of the learning process that students have lost the focus. They do the work but do not connect these details to anything meaningful to them. But when students get challenged with age-appropriate, cognitively complex tasks that connect to their world, they feel respected and valued, and they respond with creativity and excitement.

Learning outside of school often takes place in a very meaningful environment, and we store our new knowledge in multi-layered "compartments" of our brain. Picture a new experience you had recently in which you felt that you made leaps in your own learning. What music was playing at the time? What were the colors that surrounded you? What were you feeling at the time? Did you taste or smell or touch something that is a memory stored with the experience? A rich cognitive experience is always tapping multiple intelligences (Gardner, 1983; Kagan

& Kagan, 2001), and deep, permanent knowledge is stored in the brain through these cognitively complex memories. In school we reach these higher levels of acceleration of the learning process when we create rich experiences that reflect the natural process of learning experienced in hands-on tasks in family life or in the community.

Promoting cross-cultural experiences

While stimulating cognition through age-appropriate tasks, another critical key to schools that really work is to connect to students' cross-cultural life outside of school. When students can understand real-life connections to the curriculum, have actually experienced some of those connections, and can apply them to their daily life, they get excited about learning. Learning has meaning and focus. Cross-cultural explorations give great depth to the learning process and stimulate multiple intelligences, if these experiences are done thoughtfully and sensitively. The Internet is now an incredible learning tool, connecting all regions of the Earth. When teachers explore a theme by including life experiences shared by all the diverse backgrounds that students bring to the classroom, the theme reaches new levels of complexity and wonder. Teachers and students together grasp new ways of looking at life, fresh perceptions, and creative responses which can lead to inventive and cooperative solutions to some of the challenges of life in the 21st century.

Developing two languages

Thematic units taught through both languages in a spiraling curriculum naturally lead to cross-cultural sharing. In a bilingual school, each instructional language must be developed to a deep level of academic proficiency, for all subjects. Teams of teachers across adjacent grade levels can plan instructional patterns so that every subject area is covered through meaningful thematic units, with thoughtful design of what will be taught in each language. The material in one language reinforces, but does not repeat, that learned in the other language. Students know that they must pay close attention, whether they are working in their first or second language, for they are developing their ability to do grade-level work across the curriculum in both languages.

Using Spanish as an example of the non-English language, both Spanish language arts and English language arts are taught through meaningful academic content, not through isolated language lessons. The old ways of teaching language by memorizing isolated vocabulary words and teaching grammar points out of context are passé. Instead, students engage in collaborative learning that focuses on the social construction of meaning, with listening, speaking, reading, and writing taught as an integrated whole within the context of exciting academic content.

Visionary schools

A new middle school. So let's make a dream come true by trying out one vision. Or maybe this glimpse gives you some concepts to explore. We're in a small city in North Carolina, surrounded by rural agriculture, where workers have been so badly needed that many families have emigrated there from rural Mexico and Central America. The school system has grown very quickly, with local demographics shifting from mostly white and African American students to 40% Latino over a 10-year period. Finally, the school district receives funding to build a new middle school, and the architect develops a plan based on some architectural ideas from Mexico that includes a very large school courtyard, surrounded by classrooms with lots of windows and classroom doors facing the courtyard, as well as using principles of green building, with energy-efficient systems using solar and wind power and rainwater harvesting. The new bilingual principal and staff decide to start the first year with a theme for all the classes, through which all subjects will be taught. The theme is Permaculture (creating ecologically sound, healthy, sustainable, interconnected systems of living harmoniously with the natural world), and the courtyard will become a key student work area for developing experimental permaculture gardens that will serve some of the needs of the surrounding community.

Two of the three feeder elementary schools for this middle school have developed two-way bilingual classes, so that half of the student body has received PK-5 schooling through Spanish and English, including some native English speakers. Because of this mix of students, the middle school provides some classes in Spanish, while other classes are taught in English. The bilingually-schooled students are encouraged to continue to enroll in several courses taught in Spanish. Newly-arrived Spanish-speaking students who have little proficiency in English are also strongly encouraged to enroll in the courses taught in Spanish, and they are provided with intensive ESL content classes for the remainder of their school day.

The staff chosen for this middle school take a course in permaculture, and they participate in a summer institute before the middle school opens to experiment with curricular connections to the theme, across all subjects. They watch a documentary demonstrating some of the principles of permaculture and sustainability, *The Power of Community: How Cuba Survived Peak Oil*, and gather resources from new permaculture techniques for backyard ecosystems based on nature's organic principles as well as sources of wisdom from indigenous peoples of all the Americas. Through the Internet, they examine sources of permaculture information that might connect their school to other schools in Mexico and Central America that have developed methods of organic gardening and green energy systems for school buildings.

In the fall of 2001, after lengthy research and planning processes, Grandview School District implemented a two-way dual language program. The research findings of the Collier/Thomas work were the catalyst for the design and implementation of our program. ... Throughout the process of implementation, I found there to be many complexities that continue the need for refinement of approaches and strategies. I created a district-wide team of key stakeholders: superintendent, principals, ELL coaches, mainstream teachers, and dual language teachers. the purpose and role of this team was to build a common understanding of the complexities of Grandview School District's dual language program ... These stakeholders help build bridges in my efforts to reach the tipping point of common understanding and support throughout the district. However, I believe the real stakeholders that help build capacity are our students.

"It's easy. I already know how to read half in Spanish and almost every word in English. It helps me when I go over to my grandma's house. She doesn't speak very much English, so sometimes I have to help her."
Marlene, first grader

"I like learning in two languages because it will help me get a better job, and for the people that only speak one language, I can help them because I can speak two languages."
Stephanie, fifth grader

MINERVA MORALES
ASSISTANT SUPERINTENDENT
GRANDVIEW SCHOOL DISTRICT
GRANDVIEW, WASHINGTON

As school starts, students and faculty work together to experiment with their curricular goals, knowing that everyone is learning together. The whole school understands that their interaction with the natural world that develops in their mini-ecosystems inside the courtyard will change from month to month, but they are responsible for creating permanent ecosystems in the courtyard that can serve as a laboratory for the whole community. The school becomes a resource to the families and surrounding community on avoiding toxins in the environment, simple systems for sustainability, recycling, saving energy, growing healthy organic food, and knowledge of local birds, insects, mammals, plants, and their relationship to the natural ecosystems of the region.

An urban high school. Now let's travel across the country to a large west coast city. The school district is very large and the student population multilingual. Many students were born in the city, and at the same time, new immigrants arrive every day from many countries around the world. Over 75 languages are represented among the diverse students attending these urban schools.

The school district chooses five high schools that will serve as magnet bilingual/bicultural campuses for the five largest language groups represented among the student population. One of those chosen languages is Mandarin Chinese. The Chinese-English high school begins by developing the bicultural resources that will become part of their curriculum, with the bilingual staff participating in year-long preparations and an intensive summer institute. They choose a partner school in Beijing with whom they propose a long-term relationship and technological resources to communicate between the two schools. Some curricular units are planned in English and others in Mandarin Chinese that will be jointly shared by the two schools. When appropriate, student projects may be exchanged. Students in the two schools teach each other, by advising through email and websites. Ideas for using the Internet for bilingual/bicultural learning come from *Brave New Schools: Challenging Cultural Illiteracy through Global Learning Networks* by Jim Cummins and Dennis Sayers (1995), and *Language Magazine* (August, 2009) among many other references.

Satellite communications allow art, music, drama, athletic, and dance performances in both schools to be transmitted across the ocean to the partner school. Geography and anthropology units lead to cross-cultural studies that analyze relationships across the two countries. As students continue to develop deeper and deeper academic proficiency in the two languages of instruction, they establish friendships that lead to travel and cross-cultural exchanges with families during school vacations. In Chinese and English linguistics classes, the students fine-tune their language arts knowledge of their first and second languages. Literature is carefully chosen to help students reflect on cross-cultural issues, including Chinese-American literature written by Chinese immigrants to the United States. As students and teachers together reflect on the business world and global markets, they analyze current and future relationships between our two countries, understanding the needs and concerns of both countries and exploring future possibilities.

The five magnet high schools of this large city become so popular that they eventually have waiting lists for students eager to attend. After demonstrated success with the first five high schools, the school board commits to open more magnet high schools of this type and graduate many more students with bilingual/biliterate/bicultural proficiency in English and another language. Student graduates often receive scholarships to prestigious universities because of their giftedness due to developing deep proficiency in two languages. They travel with confidence to other countries, and they become resources for their community, both in the professional world and their personal lives.

An elementary school, Grades PK–5. In the middle of large farmlands in the central U.S., located in a region not accustomed to substantial immigration, a need for laborers in the food processing industry has led to a dramatic increase in indigenous families emigrating from a region of rural Mexico that is economically poor, in the state of Michoacán. Initially, the teachers in the elementary school serving this growing population receive some training in ESL techniques. But they quickly become overwhelmed with the numbers of new students arriving from Mexico who have not had the opportunity to attend school before. Adding a few bilingual staff members doesn't change students' academic performance dramatically. After several years of falling test scores, the staff decides to try something really different. They have heard of dual language schooling, and they know a school in their state that they can visit to observe this model in action. The visit excites the teachers, and they decide to try something new and different—a trilingual school.

For the three- and four-year-olds, the students of Mexican Indian origin experience hands-on learning through their primary language, Mixteco. A few mothers in the community have been hired as preschool teachers to develop cognitive skills in Mixteco through songs, games, cooking, and native cultural experiences. During the Spanish instructional time, these students extend their oral Spanish language development with native English speakers who participate in hands-on discovery learning classes for a portion of the school day. By kindergarten, both English- and Mixteco-Spanish-speaking students are beginning to experience reading and writing in Spanish. Literacy in English is introduced in first grade, and from that point on, the school curriculum is taught through Spanish and English. Mixteco experiences continue in after-school opportunities developed by families in the community.

In Señora Martínez's first grade class, the students work together developing geometric patterns with origami, writing stories for a bilingual magazine, growing organic plants from both the U.S. and Mexico that they eat, caring for some beloved class pets that come from their neighborhood, mastering math concepts through hands-on realia, reading authentic children's literature, and tackling social studies topics from a bicultural perspective. With this and each succeeding grade, all students at the school receive half of their instructional time in Spanish and half in English, taught by teacher teams. New arrivals join the classes of their age group and are paired with bilingual buddies and given extra support in after-school and weekend activities.

Some of the Spanish-speaking teachers were recruited from the region in Mexico from which the new arrivals emigrated. All teachers at the school get planning time for working in their teams as well as intensive staff development in Guided Language Acquisition Design (*Project* GLAD®), Sheltered Instruction Observation Protocol (SIOP), cooperative learning, and other innovations for teaching through first and second languages (Echevarría, Short & Vogt, 2008; Kagan, 2001; McMann & Meyer-Jacks, 2009; Vogt & Echevarria, 2006).

The most exciting changes in the school come with family activities. Both English-speaking and Spanish-speaking families come to view the school as their home away from home. After experiencing initial reticence, both groups increasingly participate in many after-school and weekend events. Some parents establish evening classes at the school to experience teaching each other some uses of Spanish and English in their familial contexts and to exchange knowledge. A few

English-speaking families decide to plan a summer visit to the region of origin of the families from Mexico. That trip leads to sending a work group to assist with building a community school needed in a small town in Michoacán. Teachers from the school join these trips, collecting authentic materials in Spanish for their classes. They attend bilingual education conferences in Mexico and the U.S. and help set up information exchanges.

Visualizing your own dream school

So many possibilities emerge when we think creatively, reflecting on new ways to stimulate cognition that connect to students' lives outside of school and make use of the linguistic and cultural resources within our own community and beyond. Knowledge explosion in the 21st century is accelerating at such a rapid pace that there is no way that teachers can know everything. So the key is to give teachers the opportunity to explore knowledge building with our students. First we engage students in the foundations of learning—reading, writing, and mathematics concepts—through meaningful curricular activities that connect our students to their world outside of school. Then we expand their understandings of the sciences, social studies, health, art, music, movement, athletics, technology, and all aspects of life through explorations together in meaningful bilingual/bicultural thematic units (Rosebery & Warren, 2008). Teachers work in teams, gathering the resources for the school curriculum. Students can work with teachers in both developing the units and gathering the resources.

When the curricular units focus on solving major community concerns, the students develop motivation. They can see the connections to what their families and others talk about. Students develop pride and responsibility for their ability to study a problem, synthesize information, analyze, evaluate, and make decisions. As the units expand to the broader world, students can see that their problem-solving abilities can be applied to larger and larger contexts.

Language develops best through the use of each language in meaningful contexts. As students' language systems expand, their cognition expands. In the long term, students develop new pathways in the brain, new brain functions, and thus they expand the uses of their brains for creative problem-solving. Bilinguals excel at creativity and divergent thinking (Baker, 2006, 2007; Bialystok, 1991, 2001; Díaz & Klingler, 1991; Tokuhama-Espinosa, 2000, 2003).

So go for it! Create your visionary schools! Don't let the politics of the past keep you from your dreams. Visualize the future. Use the research knowledge base to inform practice. Analyze where you are now, and plan creatively. Our students will take us to a new future.

Reflections from the Field

I have found that communities that have experienced success in two-way dual language education have understood the magnitude of leadership in bringing people together to interact in conversations that cultivate a common language of responsibility and commitment. It is a reform movement that takes shape as a result of those conversations. Two-way dual language programs across the country are never exactly the same—and they should not be! These are not packaged or scripted models of education that are replicated. They evolve as the leadership in these educational communities draws on their specific resources and needs to meet the goals of two-way dual language education.

... Genuine leadership inspires a profound understanding of diversity as children, teachers, parents, and the wider education community learn, work, and play together. It embraces the value of knowing more than one language and expects nothing less than a rigorous curriculum delivered and learned in two languages. As a result, these communities have not only implemented successful two-way dual language programs, but as a result of their leadership, they have accomplished the more difficult task—sustainability!

Dr. Elena Izquierdo
University of Texas at El Paso
El Paso, Texas

CHAPTER EIGHT: ACTION RECOMMENDATIONS

Based on our collaborative data collection and data analyses, we have made the following recommendations to each of the school systems with whom we have jointly engaged in action-oriented research over the past 25 years. We pass on these recommendations to other school systems, based on our findings and those of many other researchers in the field.

Action 1: Don't "water down" instruction for English learners and don't completely separate them from the instructional mainstream for many years; but also don't dump them into the mainstream unassisted until they are ready to successfully compete with native English speakers when taught in English. English learners need on-grade-level instruction in their first language while they are learning English, the same cognitive development opportunities as native English speakers receive, and continued assistance after they enter the regular instructional program.

Action 2: Provide opportunities for parents to assist their children using the parents' first language—the one they know best and in which they can best interact with their children at a higher cognitive level. Parents, even those with little education, can help you with their children's cognitive development at home. With help from you, they can assist in their children's academic development at home as well. This can help prevent the cognitive and academic slowdown that can occur when students are taught exclusively in English at school. In this way, parents can provide additional first language support which helps English learners keep up with their native-English-speaking peers' rate of cognitive and academic progress while they are learning English. Parents can also provide a learning microcosm that is favorable toward their first language, thus giving their children the documented advantages of an additive bilingual environment, even if the school represents a subtractive environment.

Action 3: Provide continuing cognitive and academic development while your students are learning English by means of the use of their first language in instruction for a part of each school day. Both languages can be developed each instructional year. But students need to reach full development of their first language in order to fully develop their second language, English. Don't let them experience cognitive slowdown or academic slowdown, relative to the native English speakers, while they are acquiring English to a level necessary to successfully compete with the native English speakers on academic tasks and tests in English on grade level.

Action 4: Use current approaches to instruction, emphasizing interactive, discovery learning and raising the cognitive level of instruction in all classrooms by avoiding "drill and kill" programs that may have positive short-term effects but which fail to allow students to sustain their achievement gains across time and to reach full parity with native speakers of English. Students working cooperatively together in a socioculturally supportive classroom do better than those taught traditionally. Provide ongoing staff development for teachers to share and co-develop cooperative learning, thematic lessons, literacy development in both first and second languages across the curriculum, process writing, performance and portfolio assessment, uses of technology, multiple intelligences, critical thinking, learning strategies, and global perspectives infused into the curriculum.

Action 5: Improve the sociocultural context of schooling for all of your students, English learners and native English speakers alike. This means that your school should become an additive bilingual environment, viewing bilingualism as enrichment, even while your community may represent a highly subtractive language-learning environment. In a socioculturally supportive school, all students and staff and parents are respected and valued for the rich life experiences in other cultural contexts that they bring to the classroom. The school is a safe, secure environment for learning, and students treat each other with respect, with less expression of discrimination, prejudice, and hostility.

Action 6: If, for pragmatic and practical reasons (e.g., a low-incidence language or shortage of bilingual teachers), you must use all-English instruction, select and develop its more effective forms. Specifically, try to move your school away from its least effective form, ESL pullout, and move toward the use of ESL taught through academic content and current approaches to teaching as a more efficacious alternative that helps students develop academically and cognitively to a greater degree. Develop your ESL content program fully over the next 3 to 5 years by engaging all mainstream and bilingual/ESL staff in professional development activities that increase their understanding of the theory and teaching practices associated with this program, so that you improve the degree to which it is fully and faithfully implemented. Your goal is to try to close some of the "second half" of the English learners' achievement gap that typical ESL content classes do not close.

Action 7: If you are now implementing transitional bilingual education at elementary school level, try to move toward an alternative that is even more effective in the long-term—one-way or two-way dual language education. Although a well implemented transitional bilingual program is associated with significantly higher long-term achievement than ESL content, neither program closes the achievement gap between English learners and native English speakers in the long term. Dual language programs can be implemented using your present bilingual teachers, and providing them with intensive staff development. But the enriched program features represent an improved and enhanced form of transitional bilingual education.

Action 8: If many of your English learners qualify for free and reduced lunch, a measure of low socioeconomic status, implementing a dual language program reduces the impact of poverty dramatically, so that your students of all socioeconomic backgrounds can succeed in school. This is equally true for your native English speakers who come from poverty (Lindholm-Leary, 2001; Thomas & Collier, 2002). One-way and two-way dual language programs provide mainstream, enrichment bilingual schooling, allowing all students to eventually reach full educational parity with native English speakers in your school.

> ... We are beginning to see that the years and effort we have invested in improving our Spanish component are beginning to pay off. Through program evaluation, constant communication, constructive criticism, and collaboration, we strive to provide our students with the best bilingual immersion experience we can offer.
>
> MARLENY PERDOMO
> ARLINGTON PUBLIC SCHOOLS
> ARLINGTON, VIRGINIA

Action 9: If you are now implementing two-way or one-way dual language education, work on more fully developing a valid and effective implementation of this approach. There are three non-negotiable components of this model: (1) a minimum of 50% of instruction in the non-English language, (2) strict separation of languages, and (3) a K-12 commitment (Rogers, 2009). Plan to offer this program at both the feeder middle school and high school, for those students who received it in elementary school. A strong dual language program includes high-level academic coursework offered in both the non-English language and English throughout all the years of schooling, including courses required for graduation from high school.

Action 10: Avoid minimalist thinking and focus on program effectiveness and benefits as well as costs. When you focus on minimizing time and money spent on English learners, without considering the negative impact of such decisions, you will not close the achievement gap. Instead, you must focus on programs that maximize educational benefits, while maintaining cost efficiency. **In particular, be aware that it is most cost-effective to teach the grade-level, mainstream curriculum (not a watered-down version) to English learners and linguistically diverse students who are proficient in English by using a bilingual teacher who**

is teaching a mainstream bilingual class. The costs of this approach are the same as in any class, except for the added cost of curricular materials in two languages. ESL pullout is the least cost-effective model, because extra resource teachers are needed.

Action 11: Think enrichment rather than remediation when you design programs for English learners. Your English learners are not "broken," and they don't need fixing. What they do need is the opportunity and support to maintain their academic and cognitive development while they are enriching themselves by adding English to their own language. They have acquired their first language naturally from birth and have continued to develop this spoken language to age-appropriate level, providing them with a natural resource to assist our country, in the global community that exists today. What we all want is for English learners to be well educated and to learn English. The best and most effective way to accomplish this is to allow them to continue to develop their first language, and to use it to continue their cognitive and academic development, while they are learning English to a level commensurate with that of a native English speaker. If they can end their schooling with strong cognitive development, high academic development, a native-speaker command of English, as well as well-developed first language, so much the better! They will enrich themselves and our society by doing so.

Two languages are better than one—for English learners and for native English speakers alike. Learning two (or more) languages is the hallmark of the educated person, and is encouraged in the academic circles of the college-bound high school student and in higher education. Why not bring the enrichment advantages of learning two languages to a wider circle of students, including linguistically diverse students as well as native English speakers?

Action 12: Close that achievement gap and keep it closed! Your students deserve no less. Fret less about what is politically expedient. Stop worrying about how to compare programs with experimental precision, and be more concerned about what instructional practices will reduce the large achievement gap that presently exists between your linguistically diverse students and your native English speakers. It is probable that many (if not most) of your linguistically diverse students were born in this country, and their rights as citizens include the right to equal educational opportunity in the form of full educational parity with their native-English-speaking peers. For this to occur, you the educator must investigate what's working and what's not working for English learners as they move through the school years. You must inquire as to the long-term outcomes of your instruction and be prepared to change your strategies and practices to achieve better long-term results for your students. You must be prepared to effectively implement your chosen instructional strategies, so that you can compare well-implemented alternatives, rather than poorly implemented ones.

Do the right thing, as your best professional judgment defines it, to assure that linguistically diverse students' success in school will lead to their becoming fully productive citizens. When today's baby boomers begin to retire in droves a few years from now, your students will assume society's burdens. In our own personal enlightened self-interest, and in the interest of our nation's welfare in the early 21st century, let's make sure that by the year 2030, 40% of the nation's school-age population—our linguistically diverse students—will be ready.

Voices from the Field

Some people choose to be bilingual. For others, however, bilingualism (or multilingualism) is a part of everyday life and a part of a person's identity. Whether it's growing up in a border city along the frontera or simply being born to parents whose first language is not English, language is just as much a part of a person's culture as anything else.

My father was born and raised in Mexico while my mother was born and raised in Japan. As a kid, I remember growing up in El Paso, Texas, and hearing English, Spanish, and Spanglish spoken ubiquitously with ease by both the educated and uneducated members of my community.

My formal exposure to languages however came in fourth grade when I transferred to Alicia R. Chacón International Language Magnet School, which offered an immersion program that helped me learn the "academic English" I needed to succeed in school, while developing the Spanish I spoke at home. Additionally, the program offered a third language option of German, Russian, Japanese, or Chinese, which was something my low income community had never seen before. Now, as a Social Anthropology major at Harvard University my interest has turned to understanding the relationship between culture, language and the human mind. More specifically, I believe exposure to more than one language capacitates the mind to recognize and value diversity. Without a doubt, my involvement with dual language programs throughout the years has allowed me to better understand others and ultimately see how we as individuals create the different layers and colors of our human experiences.

KOOK-YOUNG BENITO NISHIZAWA RODRÍGUEZ
HARVARD UNIVERSITY
2006 GRADUATE, DEL VALLE H.S.,
YSLETA INDEPENDENT SCHOOL DISTRICT
EL PASO, TEXAS

APPENDIX A:
STATE TESTS, PERCENTILES, AND NORMAL CURVE EQUIVALENTS

State vs. nationally normed tests of achievement

Throughout our research since 1985, we have analyzed student test data from both state tests and from nationally normed tests. In the past decade, state tests (usually in the form of standards-based tests, criterion-referenced tests, or mastery tests) have become much more common as part of the requirements imposed by the *No Child Left Behind* legislation of 2001. State tests offer an improved focus on the specifics of the local and state curriculum, and so the content of such tests can vary greatly from state to state. For each student and subject area, these tests typically provide a raw score (number of correct answers) and a scale score (a conversion of a student's raw score on the test or a version of the test that allows students to be compared on the same scale). These scores should increase over time, and over versions of the test, as the students' number of correct answers increases. As students' raw scores meet pre-defined levels of mastery called cutoff scores (e.g., a raw score of 30 out of 40 might be defined as mastery of a given curricular area), student mastery scores (e.g., "partially mastered," "mastered," "fully mastered") are also provided for each curricular sub-area.

Decisions at the state level as to what the cutoff score should be for each grade level vary greatly from state to state, and the nature of the test content can also vary, reflecting differences among various local and state curricula. In addition, some state tests are relatively easy in comparison to other more difficult state tests. So, comparing test scores from one state's test to the scores from another state's test is virtually impossible, because of the many differences in content, average item difficulties, and definition of student mastery that exist among the states. These differences have made it quite difficult for the U.S. Department of Education to apply the intent of NCLB uniformly across the states.

In contrast to state tests, nationally normed or norm-referenced tests (NRTs) contain test content that reflects curricula and textbook series that are used nationally, or at least in many states. Thus, the content of NRTs may not exactly fit the curricular emphases of any one state. But NRTs attempt to assess curricular emphases that apply across many states. Some describe this as assessing the "mythical national curriculum" that is largely defined by merging the curricula of the larger, more populous states with the content of the textbook series that are sold in most, if not all, of the states. This type of test was common prior to the 1990s, but has been largely replaced by standards-based tests administered by the states, especially since the inception of NCLB in 2001. Norm-referenced tests also provide raw scores and scale scores for each subtest, and in addition, they typically offer national percentile scores, and perhaps grade-equivalent scores (although these have fallen out of favor for valid psychometric reasons).

The test items of an NRT typically have greater variation in difficulty than do the items on a state mastery test. In other words, an NRT is designed to "spread students out" on a continuum to facilitate comparisons of one student with the entire range of students. In addition, NRTs contain more difficult items overall than do many state mastery tests that may have a "ceiling effect," observed when many students score at or near the maximum possible score. Many of these top-scoring students could have scored even higher if the mastery test had contained more difficult items. This ceiling effect (an artificial lowering of the high scorers' observed scores) can lead educators to underestimate the true size of an achievement gap between native English speakers and English learners, for example. Thus, a norm-referenced test will typically allow the high scorers to score as high as they can, showing the full size of the achievement gap between two groups, rather than presenting a compressed estimate of the gap caused by the ceiling effect of many state mastery tests.

In some of the states in which we have conducted research, our school district collaborators decided to administer both a norm-referenced test and the state mastery test to their students. Thus, we were able to compare the two tests on the same group of students. We noted with considerable interest that, at least in one state, it was possible for students to reach mastery on the reading subtest of the state test (i.e., to exceed the mastery cutoff score) by scoring at a level well below the national average score (50th percentile) on the norm-referenced test. In such a case, the NRT would indicate the presence of a substantially larger achievement gap between native English speakers and English learners than would the state test. In other words, English learners who matched the scores of native English speakers on the state test (both groups demonstrated mastery) would score substantially lower than native English speakers on the norm-referenced test—evidence of an achievement gap that remained unclosed even though both groups had passing scores on the state test. Thus, NRTs can serve a very useful function by showing the true size of the achievement gap for groups or for individual students.

In summary, both state standards-based and norm-referenced tests can provide educators with very useful information. We recommend using state tests every year (since they are typically administered in Grades 3–8 under current NCLB guidelines) and also employing norm-referenced tests at certain "key" points in the schooling of English learners. For example, administering a norm-referenced test (or at least the reading and math subtests) upon reclassifying an English learner from a remedial ESL or transitional bilingual (TBE) program to the mainstream would provide a clear indication as to whether the achievement gap for the re-classified student has really been closed or not. In our experience, the true gap is only half closed after 2 to 3 years of a remedial program. Also, it would be very useful to administer a norm-referenced test to former English learners at the end of the elementary school years (Grade 5), at the end of the middle school years (Grade 8) and toward the end of high school, in order to check on their continued gap closure compared to native English speakers under conditions of increasing cognitive complexity in the secondary years.

Relative vs. absolute measures of achievement

The scores from state mastery tests and norm-referenced tests include raw scores, scale scores, mastery scores, and percentile scores, among others. These scores fall into two major categories called absolute measures of achievement and relative measures of achievement.

A state test typically provides test scores that are absolute measures of achievement, such as raw scores, scale scores, or scores that indicate mastery or non-mastery of content areas. Absolute scores tell us when students are making progress but they do not tell us whether the students are making enough progress to keep up with their peers as they advance from grade to grade through the school years. Thus, it is quite possible for a student to "make progress" every year but end up with very low scores by the end of the school years, when compared to his/her peers who may have outgained our student each and every year of school. It is even possible for our student to make "good progress for his/her situation" every year and still end up in the bottom one-tenth of eventual graduates.

What's missing from most state tests is a measure of relative achievement. Such a measure would provide information on how each student's absolute score (e.g., raw score, scale score, mastery score) compares to the scores of all of the students who took the test. A percentile score, typically defined as the percentage of students who scored lower than each selected raw score, offers a measure of relative achievement, but few state tests offer state percentiles (a measure of a student's performance relative to other students in the state), and none offer national percentiles (a measure of a student's performance relative to other students in the same grade around the country).

For example, knowing that a student's raw score is 40 out of 60 items on the test, and that a score of 35 is necessary for mastery, are both useful items of information. But if we also know that 80% of the students taking the test scored lower than the raw score of 40, then this relative score "calibrates" the absolute score, and provides even more information by showing that this student's score is in the top

20% of all scores in the state. Clearly, we need both absolute measures, to tell us how much progress our student is making each year, as well as relative measures, to tell us whether our student's absolute progress is less than, the same, or more than the progress of his/her fellow students across the years of schooling.

NCEs and percentiles as relative measures of achievement

In our national research on program effectiveness for English learners, we use state test scores when working with school districts within one state. However, when we are comparing the performance of English learners in various program types across the states, we mostly use nationally normed tests by necessity, because state tests cannot be readily compared from one state to another. Norm-referenced tests allow us to compare the various English learner programs across different state curricula, and they also allow us to measure the full extent of the achievement gap for English learners. In our research, the scale scores from norm-referenced tests provide a means of comparing student performance across the years in a given subject (e.g., reading, math) and the percentile scores from norm-referenced tests allow us to compare English learners in various programs with their native English speaker counterparts. However, we do use a "transformed" version of percentiles, called normal curve equivalents (NCEs), instead of the percentiles themselves.

Why? We do so in order to follow long-standing federal education regulations that specify the use of NCEs rather than national percentiles for comparing programs and student groups on norm-referenced achievement tests. There are very good reasons for this requirement, which also define psychometric reasons for preferring NCEs over percentiles.

Let's examine percentiles and NCEs more closely. Percentiles are similar to NCEs in several ways: they both range from 1–99 and they both have an average score of 50. Also, they both measure relative achievement when used in a pretest-to-posttest comparison. A student must make a full year's progress to maintain his/her initial percentile score over a 1-year period (e.g., a student who scores at the 50th percentile or 50th NCE at the end of fourth grade and scores again at the 50th percentile/NCE at the end of fifth grade has made 1 full year's progress).

So, a student who initially scored at the 50th NCE or percentile in the spring of 2008 must make 1 year's progress in 1 year's time to stay at the 50th NCE when tested a year later in the spring of 2009. Why? Because the entire group of comparison students (called the norm group in a norm-referenced test) has moved ahead in achievement during the year. This comparison group represents a "moving target" that is constantly advancing in tested achievement. Our student at the 50th NCE must also make 1 year's progress in 1 year's time to keep up with constantly advancing peers and maintain that 50th NCE score by the standards of 1 year later.

Thus, a year-to-year gain of 0 NCEs means that our student has made a year's progress in a year's time. A gain of 1, 2, 3 or more NCEs means that the student has outgained comparable peers by making more than typical amounts of progress. A 5-NCE gain (about the maximum one might expect to observe for a large group in 1 year) might be roughly equivalent to as much as 15 months' gain in a 10-month school year.

NCEs explained

So what exactly is an NCE and how is an NCE different enough from a percentile to justify its preferential use? Simply put, an NCE is a percentile that has been "transformed" to fix a serious problem of percentiles. **The problem is that percentiles are ranks, so they vary in size (and the amount of achievement they represent) depending upon where they fall in the distribution of scores.** Since they change in size, percentiles cannot be added or subtracted from each other—using them for comparisons is like using a rubber ruler. Here's an example. If the range of scores in a normal distribution is divided into equal-sized standard deviations, the five percentile difference between percentiles 1 and 6 represents about three fourths of a standard deviation. However, another 5 percentile difference, between percentiles 45 and 50, represents only about one eighth of a standard deviation. This means that a 5 percentile difference is a completely different amount of achievement depending on how high or low the percentile value is! Percentiles are smaller in the middle of the normal distribution (where about 34 percentiles fit in one standard deviation) than they are in the extremes of the normal distribution (where only about 2 percentiles fit in one standard deviation) precisely because there are more test scores clustered in the middle of the normal distribution than in the extremes. This pattern can be seen in Figure A.1, an example of a normal curve distribution of test scores, as measured in NCEs and percentiles.

In this example, the achievement difference between percentiles 1–6 is about six times larger than the achievement difference between percentiles 45–50. In other words, the actual amount of achievement represented by one percentile changes as one moves across the possible percentile values of 1 to 99. Percentiles are really ranks (e.g. first, second, third) and the achievement difference between consecutive ranks changes as one moves up or down the ranks from 1–99. We experience this phenomenon of differing distances between ranks in the real world when we remember that the first place finisher in a race (rank 1) may finish 1 foot ahead of the second place finisher (rank 2) but 100 feet ahead of the third place finisher (rank 3). In this example, using percentiles is similar to using the 1-2-3 ranks. In contrast, using an equal-interval score such as an NCE is similar to measuring the distance between finishers in feet, an equal-interval unit of measurement that shows the true distance between runners 1 and 2 (1 foot) and between runners 2

Figure A.1

Normal Curve Equivalents and Percentiles

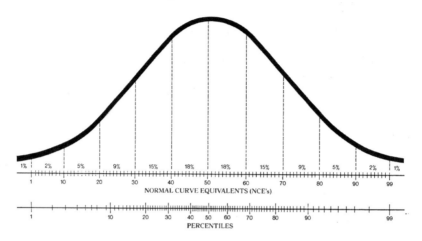

Note that percentiles are "scrunched" together in the middle of the distribution, reflecting the fact that about 68% of the scores in a normal distribution are found within one standard deviation above and below the mean score of 50. Also, note that percentiles are "stretched" at the tails (far left and far right) of the normal distribution, reflecting the fact that fewer scores are found in these ranges.

Percentile to NCE Conversion Table

%tile	NCE	%tile	NCE	%tile	NCE	%tile	NCE	%tile	NCE
1	1	21	33	41	45	61	56	81	68
2	7	22	34	42	46	62	56	82	69
3	10	23	34	43	46	63	57	83	70
4	13	24	35	44	47	64	58	84	71
5	15	25	36	45	47	65	58	85	72
6	17	26	36	46	48	66	59	86	73
7	19	27	37	47	48	67	59	87	74
8	20	28	38	48	49	68	60	88	75
9	22	29	38	49	49	69	60	89	76
10	23	30	39	50	50	70	61	90	77
11	24	31	40	51	51	71	62	91	78
12	25	32	40	52	51	72	62	92	80
13	26	33	41	53	52	73	63	93	81
14	28	34	41	54	52	74	64	94	83
15	28	35	42	55	53	75	64	95	85
16	29	36	42	56	53	76	65	96	87
17	30	37	43	57	54	77	66	97	90
18	31	38	44	58	54	78	66	98	93
19	32	39	44	59	55	79	67	99	99
20	32	40	45	60	55	80	68		

and 3 (100 feet). It is valid to say that the second interval (100 feet) is 100 times the first interval of one foot only when measuring in an equal-sized unit (in this case, feet). Since percentiles do not qualify as an equal-sized unit of measurement across their range of use, we should not add or subtract percentiles. In fact, we shouldn't even talk about raising scores by 5 percentiles as if that amount was always the same amount of achievement.

Another way to conceptualize the use of percentiles is to imagine trying to measure distance with a yardstick that is constantly changing in size as one uses it. This creates assessment havoc in interpreting measurements. Educators, school board members, and newspaper journalists who add and subtract percentile scores when comparing the test scores of groups or programs make fundamental errors of interpretation that can lead to inappropriate decisions for students in the classroom and very inappropriate policy decisions for larger groups of students.

But, we do have a legitimate need to describe relative student achievement using a score that allows us to add, subtract, or compare group achievement scores. And the percentile is very convenient for educators because it provides 99 possible distinctions (enough for almost any educational need) with an average score of 50. So, what we need is a percentile-like score whose units remain the same size from values 1 through 99. That's what a normal curve equivalent is. In Figure A.1, the scale at the bottom of the normal curve illustrates where NCEs fall on the normal curve, in contrast to percentiles, shown in the line under the NCE line.

Figure A.2 visually illustrates another way of conceptualizing the difference between percentiles and NCEs. In this figure, you can see that percentiles are ranks that vary in size; whereas NCEs are equal-interval measures.

How NCEs are computed

Testing companies who provide national NCEs in test reports have already done the statistical transformation of percentiles to NCEs for you, so you do not need to do this yourself. For example, a conversion table is provided in Figure A.1. But if you wanted to convert percentiles to NCEs yourself, as we did to produce the conversion table in Figure A.1, you could do it as follows:

Look up each percentile from 1–99 in a z-score table from a normal distribution, and write down the z-score (fraction of a standard deviation above or below the mean) that corresponds to each percentile. For example, a percentile of 9 corresponds to a z-score of -1.34, indicating that this score is 1.34 standard deviations below the mean of the distribution.

Take each z-score (remembering that z-scores represent interval data since standard deviations are the same size across the normal distribution), multiply it

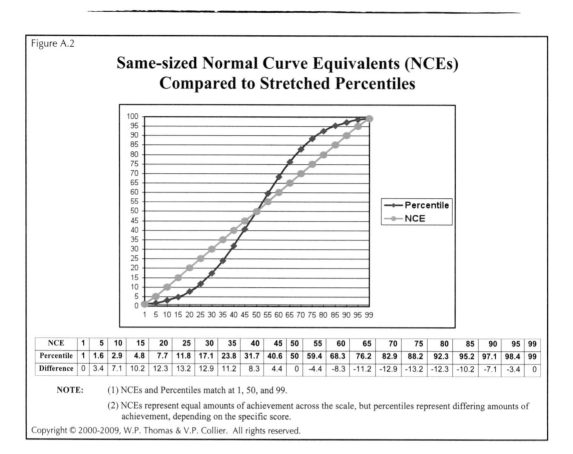

Figure A.2

Same-sized Normal Curve Equivalents (NCEs)
Compared to Stretched Percentiles

NCE	1	5	10	15	20	25	30	35	40	45	50	55	60	65	70	75	80	85	90	95	99
Percentile	1	1.6	2.9	4.8	7.7	11.8	17.1	23.8	31.7	40.6	50	59.4	68.3	76.2	82.9	88.2	92.3	95.2	97.1	98.4	99
Difference	0	3.4	7.1	10.2	12.3	13.2	12.9	11.2	8.3	4.4	0	-4.4	-8.3	-11.2	-12.9	-13.2	-12.3	-10.2	-7.1	-3.4	0

NOTE: (1) NCEs and Percentiles match at 1, 50, and 99.

(2) NCEs represent equal amounts of achievement across the scale, but percentiles represent differing amounts of achievement, depending on the specific score.

by 21.06 and add 50. In our example, a z-score of -1.34 is equivalent to an NCE of 21.8 or about 22.

Why do this? We do this because the result is a distribution of equal-sized scores from 1 to 99 with a mean of 50 and a standard deviation of 21.06. Why did we choose 21.06 as the standard deviation? Because that's what it takes to get NCE scores that range from 1 to 99, imitating percentiles. Thus, NCEs are "transformed percentiles" in that they represent percentiles that have been statistically (and legitimately so!) transformed so that the new "converted percentiles" have values from 1–99 and a mean of 50 (just like percentiles), but are equal in size across the 1–99 range of scores (unlike percentiles). Perhaps the best description of NCEs is that NCEs are really what many educators have always believed that percentiles were, but they were wrong!

How NCEs are used

Now we can add, subtract, and compare equal-sized scores from different students, from different schools, from different instructional programs, and even from different norm-referenced tests, as long as they were normed on well-selected national random samples of students, and were normed close together in time so that the random samples from each test are from the same national population of students. This is important since the characteristics of the national population and their performance on test items can change over a decade or so, requiring a re-norming of the test, usually to make it more difficult as students master curricular material at earlier and earlier ages. Since scores from norm-referenced tests that meet these criteria are based on the standards of the normal distribution, an unchanging mathematical construct, the scores from these different norm-referenced tests can be compared defensibly, at least when they are from similar time periods.

Programs that produce student achievement gains of 5 NCEs are producing gains that are equivalent to about one fourth of a standard deviation (5 NCEs divided by 21.06 NCEs in a national standard deviation). Thus, a 5 NCE gain is one fourth of a standard deviation more than the expected gain of 0 NCEs. Many program evaluators consider gains of one fourth of a standard deviation to be both statistically significant and practically significant (i.e., worthy of use in "real-world" decision-making), even for small groups of students, such as 25 students in a typical classroom.

Standards for effective instructional programs using NCEs

In our research, we look diligently for instructional programs that not only produce student achievement gains of 4–6 NCEs in 1 school year, but continue to do so, year after year. Why? First, because typical English learners in such a program will be able to close the initial 25–30 NCE achievement gap with native English speakers in about 5 to 6 years, if they demonstrate sustained NCE gains of 5 NCEs per year for 5 to 6 consecutive years. Second, an instructional program that consistently produces student achievement gains of 5 NCEs is an unusually effective program. Typical instructional programs for English learners allow these students to make gains of 0–3 NCEs. Programs of moderate-to-strong effectiveness allow typical participating students to gain from 4–6 NCEs per year more than the comparison group, which on a norm-referenced test is the national sample of mostly native English speakers. Programs of outstanding and extraordinary effectiveness allow students to gain 7–9 NCEs per year, but this level of gain is difficult to sustain over several years and is extremely rare. Figure 5.1 in Chapter 5 illustrates this pattern.

A program that shows an average annual student gain of 10 NCEs or more is somewhat suspect and requires additional examination. The gain is almost certainly caused by factors other than legitimate program effects. Such large gains can be produced when small groups are examined, since the standard error of group means is much larger for small groups of 10–25 students than for large groups of more than 100 students. Also, some tests from small test companies have ill-constructed norms and poor or non-existent random samples of the national student population, both of which can lead to NCE gains that are artificially inflated. Finally, gains above 10 NCEs per year can be incorrectly produced by accidental errors in test scoring or outright fraud. An example is using the same pre-test norms of the September testing to compare with the post-test scores in the spring. This artificially adds almost a year's achievement to each student's score. We have found that legitimate annual gains of more than 10 NCEs are virtually non-existent for large groups of students in the "real world."

This tells us that those who assert that typical English learners can reach full parity with native English speakers in 1 to 2 years are fantasizing, since this would require the typical 25–30 NCE achievement gap between these groups to be closed at the rate of 15–30 NCEs per year. It just does not happen that way for large groups of students, although a rare individual student might demonstrate this level of progress for a year or two. Average participating students will require 5 to 6 years to close the achievement gap, at average gains of 5 to 6 NCEs per year, over and above the norm group that is steadily making progress of 0 NCEs per year, which represents 1 full year's gain from the 50th NCE/percentile of fourth grade (for example) to the 50th NCE/percentile of fifth grade.

If there is to be a standard to which all programs for English learners should aspire, it is this: *All well-implemented, strong programs for English learners should allow the average participating student to reach full educational parity with native English speakers on all school subjects, tested on grade-level and in English, after 5 to 6 years of participation in the instructional program, by allowing the participating students to gain at least 5 NCEs per year, for five to six consecutive years. After parity is achieved, the school program should allow typical English learners, who are now proficient in English, to show at least the same rate of achievement gain as native English speakers (0 NCEs or more) until the end of their school years.*

APPENDIX B:
THE THOMAS-COLLIER TEST OF EQUAL EDUCATIONAL OPPORTUNITY

How is your school district doing?

Is your school system allowing its English learners to achieve parity in long-term achievement with native English speakers? You can use the *Thomas-Collier Test of Equal Educational Opportunity* to find out. Here is how it works:

Step 1: Examine your district-wide test results (norm-referenced tests, state curricular tests) in the last grade in which you test your students at the end of elementary school and high school. For example, let's assume that you administer a nationally-normed test or state curricular test in Grades 5 and 11.

Step 2: Separate out the scores of all students who have attended your school district for 5 years or more. Set aside the scores of those who have attended your schools for less than 5 years. Also do not include the scores of former English learners who arrived in your school district in the upper grades with interrupted or no previous formal schooling.

Step 3: Separate the "5-year" groups into three subgroups: those who were previously *English learners* (ELLs), those who are linguistically diverse/*language minorities* (LM) but never were classified as ELLs, and those who are native English speakers and not ELLs or LM.

Step 4: Divide the ELL subgroup into current ELLs and former ELLs for separate analyses. In the LM-never-classified-as-ELL subgroup, separate out those students who were eligible for ELL services but whose parents refused ELL services and they were placed in the English mainstream. Separate analyses should be conducted for this subgroup. Also, among native English speakers, you may want to analyze separately the test scores by ethnic categories (whites, blacks, multi-racial) and by other subgroups, such as those students receiving special education services or Title I services.

Step 5: Compute the average current 5th grade and/or 11th grade test scores for each of the three main groups (former ELLs, LM but never classified as ELLs, and native English speakers) and compare them with each groups' year-one average test scores. Use NCEs or scaled standard scores from NRTs, or scale scores from state tests, but do not use grade-equivalent scores or percentiles, since these are not equal-interval data and are misleading. See Figure B.1 for a summary of these steps and Figure B.2 for an example.

Figure B.1

Performing the Thomas-Collier Test
of Equal Educational Opportunity

Language Minority (LM) students, also called linguistically diverse students, who are in <u>strong</u> programs make gains of 4–6 NCEs per year. **At this rate of gain, even strong programs require 4–7 years to close the typical 25–30 NCE achievement gap.**

Step 1 – look at students whom you've taught for at least 5 years in your school district (e.g., Grade 5 students, Grade 11 students) and who have test scores from standard tests of grade-level achievement administered in English.

Step 2 – divide these students' scores into three main groups:

Group 1:   students who are LM and were classified as English learners (ELLs); separate these into current ELLs and former ELLs for separate analyses.

Group 2:   students who are LM but never classified as ELL; separate out any "refusers" (those eligible for but refusing ELL services) for separate analyses.

Group 3:   students who are not LM (native English speakers); separate these into ethnic or other groups (Special Education, Title I, white, black, other) for separate analyses later as needed.

Step 3 – answer the following questions using test scores:

1. At present, how large are the achievement gaps among these three main groups? Among the sub-groups?

2. Five years ago, how large were the achievement gaps among the three main groups? Among the sub-groups?

3. During the past 5 years, have your programs for ELLs allowed your former ELLs to close the achievement gaps? By how much?

The Thomas-Collier test consists of the following comparisons using the above data:

If your instructional practices are effective for native English speakers, LM students, and English learners (with typical ELLs outgaining the national norm group by about 5 NCEs per year), then your English learners should have closed the initial achievement gap with native English speakers in about 5 or 6 years. Is this the case? In other words, if your instructional practices have been effective, then former ELLs from Grade K should have closed the achievement gap with native English speakers by Grade 5 and maintained grade-level achievement at Grade 11, after both groups have received at least 5 years of schooling in your school district. When you compare the group means of (1) former English learners, (2) linguistically diverse (LM) students who were not ELLs, and (3) native English speakers, are these group means the same or within a 5-NCE range (within a year of full gap closure)? Are the means of both former English learners and linguistically diverse students who were not ELLs at or close to the 50th NCE?

If the answer is "yes," then congratulations! Your existing school practices are allowing English learners to achieve instructional parity with native English speakers in a 5-year period. This means that your instructional practices are very successful by stringent criteria, and you have passed the Thomas-Collier test that determines if English learners have received full equal educational opportunity in your school district.

If the answer is "no," then more questions are in order. Is the achievement gap in Grade 5, and also in Grade 11, smaller, the same size, or larger than it was when these students were last tested? If the answer is "larger," then your students are failing to make the "1 year's progress in 1 year's time" that is necessary for them to keep up with native English speakers. If the answer is "the same size," then your students have averaged "1 year's progress in 1 year's time" for the past several years, thus maintaining the existing gap but not closing it. If the answer is "smaller," then your students have outgained the native English speakers, but not by enough to allow them to fully close the achievement gap in the goal of 5 years. Figure B.2 gives an example of the results from one school district.

A note of caution is appropriate here. In some districts there may be substantial achievement differences among the subgroups of native English speakers, especially if there are also large subgroup differences in socioeconomic status. If so, then select the highest scoring subgroup of native English speakers and compare this group to ELLs and LM-never-classified-as-ELLs.

An Example of the Thomas-Collier Test

How are we doing? Looking at the longitudinal progress of the <u>same</u> students over a 5-year period in Total Reading:

	THEN		NOW	
Group	NCE	Percentile	NCE	Percentile
Group 1: LM students who were formerly ELL	23	10th	35	24th
Group 2: LM students who were never ELL	40	32nd	46	42nd
Group 3: Non-LM students (native English speakers)	55	59th	55	59th
Achievement Gap Summary for ELLs	**THEN:** Gap = 32 NCEs		**NOW:** Gap = 20 NCEs	

Conclusions: For former ELLs (Group 1), about one third of the gap (12 NCEs) was closed in five years at an average annual rate of 2.4 NCEs per year. Almost two thirds of the original achievement gap remains after 5 years.

You need more effective programs for ELLs in your school district.

If your school district failed the Thomas-Collier test

We have examined test data and reviewed testing summaries from school districts in more than half of the states in the U.S. during the past 25 years. *Based on this experience, we can say that a large majority of school districts have instructional practices for English learners that cause them to fall short of passing the Thomas-Collier test.* Compare our findings, summarized in Figure B.3, to your findings in your school district.

If your school district's results do not match our findings, then it is appropriate for you to examine several additional factors:

- Are there good theoretical reasons to believe that your chosen instructional practices should be effective in allowing English learners to reach eventual achievement parity with native English speakers?

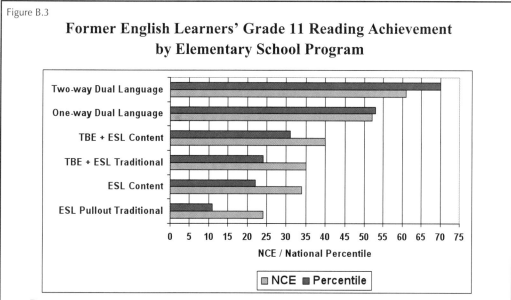

Figure B.3

Former English Learners' Grade 11 Reading Achievement by Elementary School Program

Programs:

1 - Two-way Dual Language Education (DLE), including ESL taught through academic content
2 - One-way Dual Language Education (DLE), including ESL taught through academic content
3 - Transitional Bilingual Education (TBE), including ESL taught through academic content
4 - Transitional Bilingual Education (TBE), including ESL taught traditionally
5 - English as a Second Language (ESL) taught through academic content, with no use of primary language
6 - English as a Second Language (ESL) taught by pullout from mainstream classroom, with no use of primary language

- Is your program design based on the extensive research knowledge on school effectiveness for English learners?

- For example, do your instructional practices fully address each of the components of Thomas and Collier's Prism Model?

- Is your school program well implemented?

- Are the non-negotiable features for your program clearly followed?

- Are your teachers well trained in the instructional methods that deliver your chosen programs' impact?

- Do your principals actively support the classroom instruction in their schools?

- Have all the details of implementation been carefully examined (e.g., quality curricular materials in both languages, ongoing professional development for all, enriched community relations, central office and school board support, and instructional coordination among elementary, middle, and high schools)?

- Have your programs stabilized and improved from their beginnings?

- Have you explicitly evaluated your program, visiting classrooms and schools to verify that the program design is actually being carried out?

In summary, the success of instructional programs for all linguistically diverse students depends on how well a school district addresses the major factors shown in Figure B.4.

Schools that select a theoretically powerful program, implement the program validly, thoroughly address all the dimensions of the Prism Model, create a true additive bilingual school environment, and achieve the most productive use of instructional time, are the schools that will completely close the achievement gap and more, with students excelling above grade level. In doing so, these schools become the transformed schools that meet the demands of 21st century life.

Figure B.4

What major factors influence
Language Minority (LM) program success?

(1) *The Potential Quality of LM Program Type*:

the power of a particular program's features to influence student achievement; some LM programs are feature-rich with enhanced potential to affect student achievement while others are feature-poor with little or no theoretical reason to believe that their use will help LM students close the achievement gap.

(2) *The Realized Quality of LM Program Type:*

the degree of full and effective implementation of a program in terms of administrative support, teacher skills and training to deliver the full instructional effect of the program; the degree to which program installation, processes, and outcomes are monitored and formatively evaluated.

(3) *The Breadth of Program Focus:*

an instructional focus on the Prism dimensions of cognitive, academic, and linguistic development to native-English-speaker levels in a supportive sociocultural school environment rather than a narrow and restrictive instructional focus ("just learn enough English to get by").

(4) *The Quality of the Instructional Environment:*

the degree to which the school becomes an additive language-learning environment rather than a subtractive environment, including parental engagement and support of the instructional program.

(5) *The Quality of Available Instructional Time:*

the degree to which instructional time is used effectively so that students receive maximally comprehensible instruction for an instructionally optimum time period ("more time-on-task is not necessarily better") in classrooms where ELLs interact with both ELLs and non-ELLs on a regular basis, where ELLs are not instructionally isolated, and where instruction is driven by students' cognitive, academic, and linguistic developmental needs.

Appendix C: Table of Figures

All figures from *Educating English Learners for a Transformed World* can be downloaded at *http://www.dlenm.org/educatingEnglishlearners/bookfigures* for professional development or advocacy purposes.

References

(Links to most Thomas & Collier publications and other selected publications are available at http://www.thomasandcollier.com–Research links.)

Baker, C. (2006). *Foundations of bilingual education and bilingualism* (4th ed.). Bristol, UK: Multilingual Matters.

Baker, C. (2007). *A parents' and teachers' guide to bilingualism* (3rd ed.). Bristol, UK: Multilingual Matters.

Baker, C., & Prys Jones, S. (1998). *Encyclopedia of bilingualism and bilingual education*. Bristol, UK: Multilingual Matters.

Berko Gleason, J. (2009). *The development of language* (7th ed.). Needham Heights, MA: Allyn & Bacon.

Berliner, D. C., & Biddle, B. J. (1995). *The manufactured crisis: Myths, fraud, and the attack on America's public schools*. Reading, MA: Addison-Wesley.

Bialystok. E. (Ed.). (1991). *Language processing in bilingual children*. Cambridge: Cambridge University Press.

Bialystok, E. (2001). *Bilingualism in development: Language, literacy, and cognition*. Cambridge: Cambridge University Press.

Callahan, R. M. (2005). Tracking and high school English learners: Limiting opportunity to learn. *American Educational Research Journal, 42*(2), 305–328.

Carrera, J. W. (1989). *Immigrant students: Their legal right of access to public schools*. Boston: National Coalition of Advocates for Students.

Castañeda v. Pickard, 648 F.2d 989 5th Cir. (1981).

Cazabón, M. T., Nicoladis, E., & Lambert, W. E. (1998). *Becoming bilingual in the Amigos Two-way Immersion program*. Washington, DC: Center for Applied Linguistics.

Chu, H. S. (1981). *Testing instruments for reading skills: English and Korean (Grades 1–3)*. Fairfax, VA: Center for Language and Culture, George Mason University.

Cloud, N., Genesee, F., & Hamayan, E. (2000). *Dual language instruction: A handbook for enriched education*. Boston: Heinle and Heinle.

Collier, V. P. (1987). Age and rate of acquisition of second language for academic purposes. *TESOL Quarterly, 21*, 617–641. (See http://www.thomasand-collier.com–Research links.*)*

Collier, V. P. (1988). *The effect of age on acquisition of a second language for school.* Washington, DC: National Clearinghouse for English Language Acquisition. (See http://www.thomasandcollier.com–Research links.)

Collier, V. P. (1989). How long? A synthesis of research on academic achievement in second language. *TESOL Quarterly, 23*, 509–531. (See http://www.thomasandcollier.com–Research links.)

Collier, V. P. (1992). A synthesis of studies examining long-term language minority student data on academic achievement. *Bilingual Research Journal, 16*(1-2), 187–212. (See http://www.thomasandcollier.com–Research links.)

Collier, V. P. (1995a). *Acquiring a second language for school.* Washington, DC: National Clearinghouse for English Language Acquisition. (See http://www.thomasandcollier.com–Research links.)

Collier, V. P. (1995b). *Promoting academic success for ESL students: Understanding second language acquisition for school.* Elizabeth, NJ: New Jersey Teachers of English to Speakers of Other Languages-Bilingual Educators.

Collier, V. P. (1995c). Second language acquisition for school: Academic, cognitive, sociocultural, and linguistic processes. In J.E. Alatis et al. (Eds.), *Georgetown University Round Table on Languages and Linguistics 1995* (pp. 311–327). Washington, DC: Georgetown University Press. (See http://www.thomasandcollier.com–Research links.)

Collier, V. P., & Thomas, W. P. (1989). How quickly can immigrants become proficient in school English? *Journal of Educational Issues of Language Minority Students, 5*, 26–38. (See http://www.thomasandcollier.com–Research links.)

Collier, V. P., & Thomas, W. P. (2004). The astounding effectiveness of dual language education for all. *NABE Journal of Research and Practice, 2*(1), 1–20. (See http://www.thomasandcollier.com–Research links.)

Collier, V. P., & Thomas, W. P. (2005). The beauty of dual language education. *TABE Journal, 8*(1), 1–6. (See http://www.thomasandcollier.com–Research links.)

Collier, V. P., & Thomas, W. P. (2007). Predicting second language academic success in English using the Prism Model. In J. Cummins & C. Davison (Eds.), *International handbook of English language teaching, Part 1* (pp. 333–348). New York: Springer.

Collier, V. P., Thomas, W. P., & Tinajero, J. V. (2006). From remediation to enrichment: Transforming Texas schools through dual language education. *TABE Journal, 9*(1), 23–34. (See http://www.thomasandcollier.com–Research links.)

Crawford, J. (1999). *Bilingual education: History, politics, theory, and practice* (4th ed.). Los Angeles: Bilingual Educational Services.

Cummins, J. (1976). The influence of bilingualism on cognitive growth: A synthesis of research findings and explanatory hypotheses. *Working Papers on Bilingualism, 9*, 1–43.

Cummins, J. (1981). Age on arrival and immigrant second language learning in Canada: A reassessment. *Applied Linguistics, 11*(2), 132-149.

Cummins, J. (1991). Interdependence of first- and second-language proficiency in bilingual children. In E. Bialystok (Ed.), *Language processing in bilingual children* (pp. 70–89). Cambridge: Cambridge University Press.

Cummins, J. (1996). *Negotiating identities: Education for empowerment in a diverse society.* Los Angeles, CA: California Association for Bilingual Education.

Cummins, J. (2000). *Language, power and pedagogy: Bilingual children in the crossfire.* Bristol, UK: Multilingual Matters.

Cummins, J., & Swain, M. (1986). *Bilingualism in education.* New York: Longman.

de Jong, E. J. (2002). Effective bilingual education: From theory to academic achievement in a two-way bilingual program. *Bilingual Research Journal, 26*(1), 65–84.

Díaz, R. M., & Klingler, C. (1991). Towards an explanatory model of the interaction between bilingualism and cognitive development. In E. Bialystok (Ed.), *Language processing in bilingual children* (pp. 167–192). Cambridge: Cambridge University Press

Dolson, D. P., & Lindholm-Leary, K. J. (1995). World class education for children in California: A comparison of the two-way bilingual immersion and European school models. In T. Skutnabb-Kangas (Ed.), *Multilingualism for all.* Lisse, The Netherlands: Swets & Zeitlinger.

Dulay, H., & Burt, M. (1980). The relative proficiency of limited English proficient students. In J.E. Alatis (Ed.), *Current issues in bilingual education* (pp. 181–200). Washington, DC: Georgetown University Press.

Duncan, S. E., & De Avila, E. A. (1979). Bilingualism and cognition: Some recent findings. *NABE Journal, 4*(1), 15–20.

Dutcher, N. (2001). *The use of first and second languages in education: A review of international experience* (2nd ed.). Washington, DC: Center for Applied Linguistics.

Echevarría, J., Short, D., & Vogt, M. (2008). *Making content comprehensible: The Sheltered Instruction Observation Protocol.* Boston, MA: Pearson.

Editorial Projects in Education Research Center. (2009). *Education Week, 28*(17), 1–54.

Freeman, D. E., & Freeman, Y. S. (2001). *Between worlds: Access to second language acquisition* (2nd ed.). Portsmouth, NH: Heinemann.

Freeman, Y. S., & Freeman, D. E. (2002). *Closing the achievement gap: How to reach limited-formal-schooling and long-term English learners.* Portsmouth, NH: Heinemann.

Freeman, Y. S., & Freeman, D. E. (2006). *Teaching reading and writing in Spanish and English in bilingual and dual language classrooms* (2nd ed.). Portsmouth, NH: Heinemann.

Freeman, Y. S., & Freeman, D. E. (2009). *Academic language for English language learners and struggling readers.* Portsmouth, NH: Heinemann.

García, E. (1993). Language, culture, and education. In L. Darling-Hammond (Ed.), *Review of research in education* (Vol. 19, pp. 51–98). Washington, DC: American Educational Research Association.

García, E. (1994). *Understanding and meeting the challenge of student cultural diversity.* Boston: Houghton Mifflin.

Gardner, H. (1983). *Frames of mind: The theory of multiple intelligences.* New York: Basic Books.

Genesee, F. (1987). *Learning through two languages: Studies of immersion and bilingual education.* New York: Newbury House.

Genesee, F. (Ed.). (1994). *Educating second language children: The whole child, the whole curriculum, the whole community.* Cambridge: Cambridge University Press.

Genesee, F., Lindholm-Leary, K., Saunders, B., & Christian, D. (2006). *Educating English language learners: A synthesis of research evidence.* Cambridge: Cambridge University Press.

Gold, N. (2006). *Successful bilingual schools: Six effective programs in California.* San Diego: San Diego County Office of Education. http://www.sdcoe.net/lret2/els/pdf/SBS_Report_FINAL.pdf

Goldenberg, C. (2008). Teaching English language learners: What the research does—and does not—say. *American Educator, 32*(2), 8–23, 42–44. http://www.aft.org/pubs-reports/american_educator/issues/summer08/goldenberg.pdf

González, V. (2005). Cultural, linguistic, and socioeconomic factors influencing monolingual and bilingual children's cognitive development. *NABE Review of Research and Practice, 3*, 67–104.

Greene, J. P. (1997). A meta-analysis of the Rossell and Baker review of bilingual education research. *Bilingual Research Journal, 21*(2/3), 1–22.

Grosjean, F. (1982). *Life with two languages: An introduction to bilingualism.* Cambridge, MA: Harvard University Press.

Hakuta, K. (1986). *Mirror of language: The debate on bilingualism.* New York: Basic Books.

Hargreaves, A. (Ed.). (1997). *Rethinking educational change with heart and mind.* Alexandria, VA: Association for Supervision and Curriculum Development.

Henze, R., Katz, A., Norte, E., Sather, S. E., & Walker, E. *Leading for diversity: How school leaders promote positive interethnic relations.* Thousand Oaks, CA: Corwin Press.

Hernández v. Texas, 347 U.S. 475 (1954).

Howard, E. R., & Sugarman, J. (2007). *Realizing the vision of two-way immersion: Fostering effective programs and classrooms.* Washington, DC: Center for Applied Linguistics and Delta Systems.

Jacob, E., & Jordan, C. (Eds.). (1993). *Minority education: Anthropological perspectives.* Norwood, NJ: Ablex.

Jaramillo, A., & Olsen, L. (1999). *Turning the tides of exclusion: A guide for educators and advocates for immigrant students.* Oakland, CA: California Tomorrow.

Kagan, S. (2001). *Cooperative learning.* San Clemente, CA: Kagan Cooperative Learning.

Kagan, S., & Kagan, M. (2001). *Multiple intelligences.* San Clemente, CA: Kagan Cooperative Learning.

Lambert, W. E. (1975). Culture and language as factors in learning and education. In A. Wolfgang (Ed.), *Education of immigrant students.* Toronto: Ontario Institute for Studies in Education.

Lambert, W. E. (1984). An overview of issues in immersion education. In *Studies on immersion education: A collection for United States educators* (pp.8–30). Sacramento, CA: California Department of Education.

Lau v. Nichols, 414 U.S. 563 (1974).

Lindholm-Leary, K. (1990). Bilingual immersion education: Criteria for program development. In A. M. Padilla, H. H. Fairchild & C. M. Valadez (Eds.), *Bilingual education: Issues and strategies* (pp. 91–105). Newbury Park, CA: Sage.

Lindholm-Leary, K. (1991). Theoretical assumptions and empirical evidence for academic achievement in two languages. *Hispanic Journal of Behavioral Sciences, 13*, 3–17.

Lindholm-Leary, K. (2001). *Dual language education*. Bristol, UK: Multilingual Matters.

Lindholm-Leary, K. & Aclan, Z. (1991). Bilingual proficiency as a bridge to academic achievement: Results from bilingual/immersion programs. *Journal of Education, 173*, 99-113.

Lucas, T., Henze, R., & Donato, R. (1990). Promoting the success of latino language-minority students: An exploratory study of six high schools. *Harvard Educational Review, 60*, 315–340.

McLaughlin, B. (1992). *Myths and misconceptions about second language learning: What every teacher needs to unlearn*. Santa Cruz, CA: National Center for Research on Cultural Diversity and Second Language Learning.

McLeod, B. (1996). *School reform and student diversity: Exemplary schooling for language minority students*. Washington, DC: National Clearinghouse for English Language Acquisition.

McMann, D., & Meyer-Jacks, L. (Eds.). (2009). Guided Language Acquisition Design—Integrating content, engaging students, elevating academic language and literacy. *Monographs of Dual Language Education of New Mexico*, Volume 2. http://www.dlenm.org

Moll, L. C., Vélez-Ibáñez, C., Greenberg, J., & Rivera, C. (1990). *Community knowledge and classroom practice: Combining resources for literacy instruction*. Arlington, VA: Development Associates.

Myhill, W. N. (2004). The state of public education and the needs of English language learners in the era of No Child Left Behind. *Journal of Gender, Race and Justice, 8*, 93–152. (See http://www.thomasandcollier.com–Research links.)

Oakes, J. (1985). *Keeping track: How schools structure inequality.* New Haven: Yale University Press.

Oakes, J. (1990). *Multiplying inequalities: The effects of race, social class, and tracking on opportunities to learn math and science.* Santa Monica, CA: The RAND Corporation.

Oakes, J. (1992). Can tracking research inform practice? Technical, normative, and political considerations. *Educational Researcher, 21*(4), 12–21.

Oakes, J., Quartz, K. H., Ryan, S., & Lipton, M. (2000). *Becoming good American schools: The struggle for civic virtue in education reform.* San Francisco: Jossey-Bass.

Ovando, C. J., Combs, M. C., & Collier, V. P. (2006). *Bilingual and ESL classrooms: Teaching in multicultural contexts* (4th ed.). New York: McGraw-Hill.

Parrish, T. B., Merickel, A., Pérez, M., Linquanti, R., Socias, M., Spain, A., Speroni, C., Esra, P., Brock, L., & Delancey, D. (2006). *Effects of the implementation of Proposition 227 on the education of English learners, K-12: Findings from a five-year evaluation.* Palo Alto, CA: American Institutes for Research, and San Francisco: WestEd. http://www.wested.org/online_pubs/227Reportb.pdf

Pérez, B. (2004). *Becoming biliterate: A study of two-way bilingual immersion education.* Mahway, NJ: Erlbaum.

Pérez, B., & Torres-Guzmán, M. E. (2002). *Learning in two worlds: An integrated Spanish/English biliteracy approach* (3rd ed.). Boston: Allyn & Bacon.

Plyler v. Doe, 457 U.S. 202, 102 S.Ct. 2382 (1982).

Ramírez, J. D., Yuen, S. D., Ramey, D. R., & Pasta, D. J. (1991). *Final report: Longitudinal study of structured English immersion strategy, early-exit and late-exit transitional bilingual education programs for language-minority children* (Vols. I and II). San Mateo, CA: Aguirre International.

Rogers, D. (2009). Meeting the challenge—Maintaining an effective dual language program. *Soleado: Promising Practices from the Field, 1*(4), 1, 10. http://www.soleado.dlenm.org

Rolstad, K., Mahoney, K., & Glass, G. V. (2005). The big picture: A meta-analysis of program effectiveness research on English language learners. *Educational Policy, 19*(4), 572–594.

Rosebery, A. S., & Warren, B. (Eds.). (2008). *Teaching science to English language learners: Building on students' strengths.* Arlington, VA: National Science Teachers Association.

Skutnabb-Kangas, T. (1981). *Bilingualism or not: The education of minorities*. Bristol, UK: Multilingual Matters.

Skutnabb-Kangas, T., & Cummins, J. (Eds.). (1988). *Minority education: From shame to struggle*. Bristol, UK: Multilingual Matters.

Slavin, R. E., & Cheung, A. (2003). *Effective reading programs for English language learners: A best-evidence synthesis*. Baltimore, MD: Center for Research on the Education of Students Placed at Risk (CRESPAR), Johns Hopkins University. http://www.csos.jhu.edu/crespar/techReports/Report66.pdf

Snow, C. E. (1990). Rationales for native language instruction: Evidence from research. In A. M. Padilla, H. H. Fairchild, & C. M. Valadez (Eds.), *Bilingual education: Issues and strategies*. Newbury Park, CA: Sage.

Stern, H. H. (Ed.). (1963). *Foreign languages in primary education: The teaching of foreign or second languages to younger children*. Hamburg: International Studies in Education, UNESCO Institute for Education.

Tabors, P. O., & Snow, C. (2001). Young children and early literacy development. In S. B. Neuman & D. K. Dickman (Eds.), *Handbook of early literacy research* (pp. 159–178). New York: Guilford Press.

Tharp, R. G., & Gallimore, R. (1988). *Rousing minds to life: Teaching, learning, and schooling in social context*. Cambridge: Cambridge University Press.

Thomas, W. P. (1992). An analysis of the research methodology of the Ramírez study. *Bilingual Research Journal, 16*(1-2), 213–245. (See http://www.thomasandcollier.com–Research links.)

Thomas, W. P., & Collier, V. P. (1997). *School effectiveness for language minority students*. Washington, DC: National Clearinghouse for English Language Acquisition. (See http://www.thomasandcollier.com–Research links.)

Thomas, W. P., & Collier, V. P. (2002). *A national study of school effectiveness for language minority students' long-term academic achievement*. Santa Cruz, CA: Center for Research on Education, Diversity and Excellence, University of California-Santa Cruz. (See http://www.thomasandcollier.com–Research links.)

Thomas, W. P., Collier, V. P., & Abbott, M. (1993). Academic achievement through Japanese, Spanish, or French: The first two years of partial immersion. *Modern Language Journal, 77*, 170–179. (See http://www.thomasandcollier.com–Research links.)

Thompson, M. S., DiCerbo, K. E., Mahoney, K., & MacSwan, J. (2002, January 25). Éxito en California? A validity critique of language program evaluations and analysis of English learner test scores. *Education Policy Analysis Archives, 10*(7). http://epaa.asu.edu/epaa/v10n7

Thonis, E. (1994). Reading instruction for language minority students. In C. F. Leyba (Ed.), *Schooling and language minority students* (2nd ed., pp. 165–202). Los Angeles: Evaluation, Dissemination and Assessment Center, California State University, Los Angeles.

Tinajero, J. V., & Ada, A. F. (Eds.). (1997). *The power of two languages: Literacy and biliteracy for Spanish-speaking students* (2nd ed.). New York: Macmillan/McGraw-Hill.

Tokuhama-Espinosa, T. (2000). *Raising multilingual children*. Santa Barbara, CA: Praeger.

Tokuhama-Espinosa, T. (2003). *The multilingual mind*. Santa Barbara, CA: Praeger.

Tsang, S.-L., Katz, A., & Stack, J. (2008). Achievement testing for English language learners, ready or not? *Education Policy Analysis Archives, 16*(1).

Tse, L. (2001). *Why don't they learn English? Separating fact from fallacy in the U.S. language debate*. New York: Teachers College Press.

Vogt, M., & Echevarría, J. (2006). *Teaching ideas for implementing the SIOP model*. Glenview, IL: Pearson.

Willig, A. C. (1985). A meta-analysis of selected studies on the effectiveness of bilingual education. *Review of Educational Research, 55*, 269–317.

Wong Fillmore, L. (1991a). Second language learning in children: A model of language learning in social context. In E. Bialystok (Ed.), *Language processing in bilingual children* (pp. 49–69). Cambridge: Cambridge University Press.

Wong Fillmore, L. (1991b). When learning a second language means losing the first. *Early Childhood Research Quarterly, 6*, 323–346.

Wong Fillmore, L., & Valadez, C. (1986). Teaching bilingual learners. In M. C. Wittrock (Ed.), *Handbook of research on teaching* (3rd ed., pp. 648–685). New York: Macmillan.

INDEX

A

Achievement gap/gap closure 3, 12, 19–28, 43–44, 48, 61, 64, 75–76, 81, 83–84, 102–104, 109–110, 111–114

B

Bilingualism
  Additive bilingualism 39–40, 95–96
  Bilingually schooled or bilingual schooling 2, 11, 15, 25–27, 44, 48, 65–67, 72, 75, 97
  Creativity and bilinguals, divergent thinking 75, 93
  Majority language/group 4, 33, 39, 71–72
  Minority language 4–5, 39, 71–73
  Subtractive bilingualism 39–40, 95–96

C

Cognition
  Cognitive development 32, 36–39, 41–42, 44, 49, 56, 60, 87–88
  First language cognitive development 36–39, 44, 48–49, 65, 95

D

Demographics 3–4, 9

E

Evaluation and testing
  Absolute measures 103–104
  Achievement gap/gap closure 3, 12, 19–28, 43–44, 48, 61, 64, 75–76, 81, 83–84, 102–104, 109–110, 111–114
  Criterion-referenced tests 23, 43
  Cross-sectional 11–12
  Disaggregation 11
  Longitudinal 12, 81, 83

Mastery score 101, 103
No Child Left Behind 1, 11–13
Normal curve equivalents (NCEs) 20, 42, 57, 104–110, 111
Norm group 29, 61, 104
Norm-referenced tests 43, 53, 73, 101–104, 109, 111
Percentiles 20, 103–108, 111
Raw score 101–103
Relative measures 103–104
Scale score 101–104, 111
State tests 53, 101–104, 111
Test scores 11–13, 28, 80, 101, 103–105, 107, 111–112

L

Language acquisition/development
  First language acquisition 32, 35, 37, 88
  Primary language/first language 13, 22–27, 32–33, 36–39, 48–49, 64, 79–81, 95, 98
  Second language acquisition 19–28, 31, 34–36, 37, 52, 88

N

No Child Left Behind 11–13

P

Policy
  Court decisions 10–11, 19, 60, 77, 79
  Federal legislation 1, 11–14, 16, 84, 101
  State legislation 3, 14–15, 61
Prism Model 31, 33–34, 38, 38–42, 47, 56, 58, 60, 62, 67, 116–117

Program characteristics
  Cost-effective/cost efficiency 51–52, 69, 97–98
  English-only 15, 40–42, 72
  Enrichment 24–25, 50–51, 58–59, 84, 98

Integrated 51–52, 64
Remedial/remediation 65–66, 98, 103

Programs
  50:50 73–76
  90:10 71–76
  Bilingual immersion 71
  California's Proposition 227 15,
    55–61, 72–73, 78, 83
  Dual language education 2–3, 26–27,
    52, 66–67, 71, 73–74, 96–97
  One-way 55–56, 56, 59, 66–67,
    73–74, 76, 82, 115
  Two-way 55–56, 56, 59, 60, 66–67,
    71, 73–76, 82, 89, 115
  Early-exit 66
  ESL content 55–56, 59, 63–64,
    72–73, 79–84, 96, 115
  ESL pullout 19, 55–59, 62–63,
    72–73, 82, 96, 98, 115
  Immersion 71–73
  Late-exit 66, 80
  Mainstream, role of 22, 24, 47,
    51–52, 95–98
  Structured English immersion 71–73
  Submersion 51, 71, 77–79
  Transitional bilingual education 15,
    55–56, 59, 65–66, 79–80, 82,
    96–97, 115

S

Sociocultural
  Discrimination, prejudice, hostility
    10, 35–36, 50, 65, 96
  Self-esteem 34, 42
  Social and cultural processes 96
  Social and cultural processes/support
    33–35, 42, 50–51, 65–66, 89–91
  Socioeconomic status 57, 73, 82–83,
    97, 113

Students
  Demographics 3–4, 9, 89–91

  English learners 3–6, 20, 21, 25, 27,
    40–44, 113–117
  Former English learners 5, 53, 103,
    111–115
  Language majority 4, 71
  Language minority/minorities 4–5,
    111–114, 117
  Linguistically diverse 4–6, 53, 74,
    111–113
  Socioeconomic status 57, 73, 82–83,
    97, 113

T

Teaching strategies
  Accelerated learning 51, 88
  Age-appropriate 40, 51, 87–88
  Cognitively challenging 51
  Cooperative learning 51
  Critical thinking 51
  Cross-cultural 88, 91
  Discovery learning 1, 51, 92, 96
  Global perspectives 51
  Guided Language Acquisition Design
    (*Project* GLAD®) 92
  Interactive 36, 51, 81, 96
  Multiple intelligences 51, 87–88
  Problem-solving 51
  Scaffolding 2
  Sheltered instruction 2, 63–64
  Sheltered Instruction Observation
    Protocol (SIOP) 92
  Team teaching 52
  Technology, use of 51, 91
  Thematic units/lessons 51, 88, 93
    Ecosystems 89–90
    Permaculture 89–90

Theory
  Prism dimensions 64–65, 116–117
  Prism Model 31, 33–34, 38–42, 47,
    56, 58, 60, 62, 67, 116–117
  Thomas-Collier Test 28, 68, 111–115

ABOUT THE AUTHORS

Professors Virginia Collier and Wayne Thomas are internationally known for their research on long-term school effectiveness for linguistically and culturally diverse students. Dr. Thomas is a professor emeritus of evaluation and research methodology and Dr. Collier is a professor emerita of bilingual/multicultural/ESL education, both of George Mason University. For other publications by Dr. Collier and Dr. Thomas, please visit their website at *www.thomasandcollier.com*.

ABOUT THE PHOTOGRAPHS

DLeNM extends special thanks for the photographs in this book. The following schools are represented:

Agua Fría Elementary, Santa Fe—Dr. Suzanne Jácquez-Gorman, Principal
Cien Aguas International School, Albuquerque—Mike Rodríguez, Director
Dolores Gonzales Elementary, Albuquerque—Dora Ortiz, Principal
East San José Elementary, Albuquerque—Steve Tognoni, Principal
Truman Middle School, Albuquerque—Judith Martin-Tafoya, Principal
Albuquerque High School, Albuquerque—Tim McCorkle, Principal

And our deep appreciation goes out to Anna Torres and her family for allowing us to use the black and white photograph on the front cover (and above). The teacher in that photograph is Anna's mom, who was the last teacher at the one-room schoolhouse in El Valle, New Mexico.